MW01235532

AT WAR ON THE LAFFEY

An Officer's Memoir

AT WAR ON THE LAFFEY
An Officer's Memoir

By

Kevin Cain

Other Books by Kevin Cain

This book is dedicated to the memory of Joseph Ford Cain and to all of the brave men who served and risked their lives defending the Laffey and our country all those years ago.

I also want to express my gratitude to the wonderful folks at Patriot's Point in Mt. Pleasant, SC, where the USS Laffey now rests. Thank you for caring for our "Lady."

Published by Createspace – An Amazon Company - 2017

FOREWARD

Growing up in the American south, I learned at an early age about the wonders and delights of storytelling from listening to my grandparents tell of their own life experiences. In my first book *Thanksgiving Hen on a Chicken Shed: Stories My Grandmother Told Me*, I shared the stories my own grandmother, Mildred Lee Cain, used to humor me with on summer days when I stayed with her and my grandfather (Paw-Paw as we called him) Joseph Ford Cain while I was out of school. These were stories that made me laugh, smile, thrilled me and made me want to share them over and over for others to enjoy.

While my Grandmother spun yarns about her adventures with her family in rural Alabama during the 1930's and 1940's, my Paw-Paw's stories always took a more serious note when it was his turn to share. Not only had he grown up in rural Alabama during that same time, he was also a veteran officer of the Navy who served proudly during World War II. Though many veteran's choose not to talk about the horrors they witnessed during their service in the wars, my Paw-Paw, surprisingly enough, chose willingly to share his stories with me of his adventures while serving on a destroyer, the USS Laffey, during his time in the US Navy during WW II.

At first, during my younger years, he only shared stories about the ship itself, how magnificent it was and the mechanics behind it. To hear my Paw-Paw tell it, the Laffey was like a queen on the ocean, constantly on the prowl to protect her country from enemies during those harsh years, her crew ever vigilant and caring for her every step of the way. As I grew older and matured, he began opening up about the darker side of his experience onboard this queen of the seas. As I learned, his time on Laffey was not all fun and adventure. While serving as their communications officer, he witnessed a lot of things occur that I thank God to this day that I did not have to witness myself.

World War II proved to be a bloody battle with thousands of casualties. Laffey herself saw many of those casualties occur first hand, a lot onboard her rugged deaths. The fury of the kamikaze, or "Divine Wind" as the Japanese knew them, held no mercy for our ships in their seas, and Laffey was no exception to that rule. Many ships felt the blasts of their bombs and attacks, and few returned intact. Unfortunately for him, my Paw-Paw had to witness the deaths of some of his fellow crewman. These were images that he was forced to take with him for the rest of his days.

After opening up more and more, Paw-Paw then felt comfortable enough to write down his memories of serving during WW II and his time on the Laffey, the ship that proved unsinkable. Even though he witnessed such horrid images aboard her decks, my Paw-Paw still remained nothing but proud of what he always called "that fine lady" and the service she and her crew gave forth during that time. In his mind, Laffey protected him by the grace of God, brought him through those living nightmares and tragedies and returned him safely to his family just like any good "queen" would do in the fairy tales we share with our children.

I saw Paw-Paw work for a few years on writing down what he called his memoirs. Then, one day he set them aside. When I asked him if he'd ever publish his work, he would only reply that this was more for his own therapy to finally work through what he'd witnessed and lay it all down. Someday, he told me, perhaps this might be published, but for that time being, he wanted to just let it be for himself. Once he'd finished writing what he wanted to say, he set it down and felt the relief of getting it all out.

Sometime after Paw-Paw died in October of 2014, my father and siblings went through his house to clean out his belongings, keep what we wanted and plan to sale or donate the rest. My grandmother had already passed away four years prior, so now there was no need to keep those belongings stored away. While going through the house, in a box in the top of one of their closets sat a black binder. When my father opened it, inside was my Paw-Paw's manuscript. By that time, I'd feared he had thrown the thing away sometime prior as I had not seen it in years. However, here it sat, its story still waiting to be told.

Being the writer that I am, and wanting to memorialize the stories he once told me just as I did my grandmother's before, I decided to create a book using his writings and share his story in the same words he shared them with me. When he shared his war stories with me when I was a child, to my delight, he always used sound effects for the guns and explosions, such as "Ka-Blam" and "Tat-tat-tat." So, I have also used those here in some sections of this book to add the enjoyable description for you readers.

One thing my Paw-Paw never let go of was his humble proudness for his country and our men and women in service. Even today, wars of terror still rage in our world. Even today, service men and women risk their lives every day trying to protect us, their people, here at home. My Paw-Paw never once hesitated to take his hat off to all of the service men and women who serve this country then and now. In keeping with that fashion, my hat is also off to you men and women. May God bless you and keep you safe.

Kevin Cain

The destroyer USS Laffey

The rumors are true. After many months at sea, we are going back to the states. Not the whole crew, just me. No, I am not wounded. The order sent to the USS Laffey was to transfer one senior radioman for reassignment. That senior radioman was me. Now, here I stand aboard the transport ship, a.k.a the USS Sheliak, in Buckner Bay watching as the fierce struggle for the island of Okinawa continues.

Our destroyer, USS Laffey DD724, is over there in the dead ship anchorage being kept afloat with the help of the big pumps of two sister salvage tugs. There is a sad note in my heart and, maybe, just a little guilty feeling as we get underway for Pearl harbor on the first leg of the journey home….

I, Joseph Ford Cain, am the ninth child in the family of eleven children born to Bama Arvelee Patton Cain and David Edward Cain on August 14, 1923, just south of Jasper in Walker County, Alabama. My mother is the daughter of Reverend and Mrs. William L. Patton of Patton Hill in southern Walker County. My father is the son of James Williams (Bose) Cain and was born in Texas. His parents had moved to Texas just before he was born and had lived there eleven years before returning to Walker County.

My great-grandfather James Oscar Cain, Jr. was born in Charleston, South Carolina, in 1796 to parents James Oscar Cain (an immigrant from Wales) and Joanne King Cain (of Charleston, South Carolina). In 1819, James Oscar Cain, Jr. married Elizabeth McCauley of Charleston, South Carolina, and that same year they moved to Alabama. They settled at Liberty Hill on Wolf Creek just south of what is now Oakman in Walker County territory. They entered government land in Section 24, Township 16, Range 8 and went to work.

James was active in farming, raising cattle, stave(plank)-making, ginnery (removing the seeds from cotton), coal mining, river shipping and politics. James is prominently mentioned in several books. He is given credit for opening the first underground coal mine in Walker County. He served four terms in the county legislature. During this time, he laid out the boundary lines for Walker County as they are today. At that time, Walker County territory covered what is now Walker and Winston Counties and parts of Lawrence, Cullman, Blount and Jefferson Counties. Politically, he was a whig and a powerful democrat. John Manasco was his opponent.

In rural Walker County, economically, things were not good during the Depression years. Most residents owned a country home with no electricity or running water. Food and clothing were hard to come by. As a boy, my school years were not happy ones. We walked the two and one-half miles to and from school. Had there been a school bus, we would not have been permitted to ride because we lived too close to the school to qualify. The school itself had no cooling system of any kind. Heat was furnished by one jacketed coal-burning heater in each room. There was no water system and, of course, no indoor plumbing. There was a drilled well in the school yard, but the well was dry most all the time because of underground mining. If there had been water in the well, it would not have made any difference because the kids kept breaking the pump. The children who could not bring their own water from home literally did without.

Other than a short stay in the Civilian Conservation Corp in 1943, I knew little about things outside of Walker County, Alabama. I was in the CCC camp in Florida when the Japanese attacked Pearl Harbor on December 7, 1944. In about two weeks, I was discharged from the CCC. For a few months, I worked at a coal mine. Then, World War II came close to me. My older brother Carl was in the Navy, and my older brother Linwood was in the Army Air Corps. It was now my time to join them in the battle to protect our country.

At nineteen years of age, I was still going through a bashful stage and, for several reasons that were important to me, was very, very self-conscious. Having already enlisted in the navy, I was enjoying a fifteen-days-leave before reporting to the Navy boot camp. In March of 1943, I went to a movie in the town of Townley, Alabama, and there I met the girl who would later be my wife. She had brown eyes, long and curly brown hair, five feet five inches, slightly over one hundred pounds and was two weeks short of eighteen years old. She was just about the cutest thing I had ever seen. It was a case of love at first sight. I found her name to be Mildred Lee Carrell. In my bashful and self-concious state, this would be hard to handle. But time was running out.

Mustering up what courage I could grasp, I asked her for a date. She agreed, and on a Sunday afternoon we had our first date. She had no steady boyfriend which was great for me. At the end of the date, I asked if she would date me again. She said yes! We had a few dates, but the sixteenth of April was approaching like a freight train. Micki, the nickname I later gave to Mildred, agreed to write to me while I was away, and she did so faithfully. She waited patiently and faithfully for my return, something I appreciated for the rest of my life.

On April 15, 1943, I boarded a train I Birmingham en-route to the Naval Training Station at Bainbridge, Maryland. Here, the going was rough as the Navy packed three months of training into us in only six weeks. After this came a short leave and then back to Bainbridge for assignment. I was delighted to learn that I would be attending on of the Navy's toughest radio schools, which was located at Auburn University in Auburn, Alabama. While serving in the CCC, I studied radio and communications. This proved to be very valuable. The four months at Auburn were enjoyable as I was able to make several trips home on the weekends. Not much time, but at least it meant a trip home, and that gave me uplift.

I graduated from the school with the second highest mark in the class and a third-class radioman rating. I then went from Auburn to Norfolk, Virginia, and was assigned to the crew being formed for the new destroyer…USS Laffey (DD724). While the crew was being assembled and trained, the Laffey was being completed at the Bath Iron Works located in Bath, Maine. When the ship was ready to deliver to the Navy, our crew moved up to Boston, Massachusetts. I was a member of the skeleton crew that went on to Bath, Maine, to bring the ship to Boston. This was a very exciting trip for me. I had been to sea on a training ship at Norfolk, but this was going to be *my* ship. Laffey was commissioned February 8th, 1944. Now, I was a plank owner of Laffey and much closer to the war zone.

The Laffey, a new type Sumner-class ship, was grouped with four other ships of like-class to form a destroyer division. We would work together as one unit. Training began in earnest with a shakedown cruise to Bermuda where we tested the ship and equipment at slow speed and dropped depth charges to explode shallow. In the process of the explosions, the water cooler in the

Joseph Ford Cain when he first began serving in the US Navy

USS Laffey as it appears today in Patriots Point, Mt. Pleasant, SC.

mess hall fell apart and a seam in the starboard side ripped. Everything began to look bad until the damage control people proved that they were good repairmen by bringing the Laffey to a speedy recovery. While in the Atlantic, we also experienced a strong storm during our cruise. We received a distress call stating that a PBY Flying Boat (an aircraft) had experienced trouble while flying in the storm and downed nearby our ship. We sailed to the location of the aircraft and brought the crew aboard, rescuing them from the rough waters. Because of these heroic efforts, the Laffey was chosen to visit Washington, D.C, where the crew was rewarded.

After the shakedown, we spent more time in the Navy yard for repairs and alterations followed by short cruises and more practice. At the latter part of April 1944, we entered New York for more gear and supplies. After this, we sailed on May 14, 1944. I noticed the other ships in our squadron began to gather. Something else I noticed was that these huge tankers began to appear. There were twelve in all riding low in the water, waves washing over their decks. They were heavily loaded with aviation and gasoline. We were forming a fast tanker convoy headed for England.

Now, we had lots of rumors floating around aboard ship. Radiomen are thought of to have all the information, so, when I went out on deck, all sorts of questions were directed my way. "What's up?" "Where are we going?" "Why the tankers?" "When will we arrive?" Of course, radiomen did not really have all of the information. But, since our zig-zagging course was generally east-northeast, my guess was a safe one: Europe. The invasion must be close. I prayed to God for safety and help to keep my faith alive.

On this trip, a part of my job was to man the radio direction finder, especially at night. The German submarines would surface and make radio contact at night. With my equipment, I could receive those transmissions, determine their positions in relation to our ship and pass the information to the officers on the bridge. I heard lots of German chit-chat, but nevertheless our convoy escaped attack. We released the convoy in the North Channel, English waters, and moored in Greenock, Scotland. The following day, Laffey and the other ships in our squadron along with troop transports moved south through the Irish Sea and St. George's Channel heading for Plymouth, England, on the English Channel. As we entered the open sea one day out of Plymouth, we made our first submarine contact. With the aid of our sister ship O'Brien, we made the sea foam with death charges. We were never sure of a kill, but the submarine did not bother us again. There was no more doubt of our mission. Laffey was to take part in the invasion of

Inside the radio room of the USS Laffey where Cain worked as the communications officer.

Outside the door looking into the radio room

France. Modern warships like Laffey and her sister ships Walke, Barton and O'brien just didn't waste time in the protected parts of England. Plymouth was not the end of our run. It was the beginning of a big jump to France.

Three British destroyers entered the harbor later that day, and the HMS Eskimo tied up alongside Laffey. The Eskimo's crew was made up of veterans and had the latest rumor: the invasion was less then ten days away. How right they were!

On May 29th, 1944, a security blackout was spread over Plymouth Harbor and everywhere else where people were scheduled to be involved in operation "Overlord." The invasion was scheduled for June 5th, 1944. Laffey continued to train and wait. Another destroyer arrived to strengthen our squadron. The new ships now numbered five: Barton DD722, Walke DD723, Laffey DD724, O'brien DD725 and Meredith DD726. All two-thousand, two-hundred tons with tree twin five inch mounts would become Destroyer Division 119. On May 30th, 1944, Destroyer Division 119 moved out of Plymouth Harbor for once last shore bombardment practice at Slapston Sands, a practice beach north of Dartmouth. This is the beach where, about one month earlier, German e-boats surprised a practice landing exercise, killing some seven-hundred fifty American soldiers by torpedoing the landing craft. At this time, I was not aware of the disaster. Nevertheless, we returned to Plymouth without incident.

Rumors were put to rest. The word was passed. D-Day would be June 5th, 1944. H-hour was to be 6:30 in the a.m. Laffey shipped out of Plymouth Harbor at 1:30 pm on June 3rd underway for France. By 9:00 am on June 4th, the weather had become so bad and the forecast so much worse that the whole invasion was postponed for twenty-four hours. By this time, Laffey was miles south of Portsmouth, England heading south to Normandy and riding herd on one-hundred seventy-five landing ships and craft. Did Laffey have a problem? Turn that armada without a collision! So, turn it we did. By 1:30 am on June 5th, we were in safe harbor at Weymouth, England. We didn't have long to wait. By 7:00 am that same day, Laffey was out again rounding up stragglers, putting the formation together and once again heading for the French coast and Normandy which was now one-hundred fifty miles away. The Germans had not so much as noticed because the bad weather had no doubt blinded them.

Now, D-day was June 6th and H-hour was 6:30am. Laffey was helping to support the greatest amphibious assault force the world had ever seen or would ever see. The English Channel crossing was without serious incident for our force. We were headed to "Utah Beach" (the code name for one of the five sectors of the Allied invasion of German-occupied France in the Normandy landings) and timed our arrival to coincide with the minesweepers' completion of clearing the mine fields. The sweepers went to work about 3:30 am and two hours later the German gunners were finally awakened by the exploding mines. At around 5:18 am, the German shore batteries opened fire on the British cruiser Black Prince and the U.S. heavy cruiser Tuscaloosa CA37.

Our bombardment was scheduled to begin at 5:50am. Needless to say, we began a little early. Those first targets lasted only a short time. Our bombardment group consisted of one battleship USS Nevada BB36 with ten 14" guns, heavy cruisers Tuscaloosa CA37 and Quincy CA71 with nine 8" guns each, British monitor Erebus with two 15" guns and also the British cruisers Black Prince and Enterprise. Supporting these heavies were eight American destroyers, two American destroyer escorts and the Dutch gunboat Soemba. After about fifty minutes of this bombardment, the bombers droned overhead and unloaded tons of bombs on the beach. At 6:30, H-hour, the first wave of troops began to go ashore. Laffey followed right up to the sand.

The Normandy landing area was divided into five sections. From west to east: Utah Beach, Omaha Beach, Gold Beach, Juno Beach and Sword Beach. The U.S. controlled Utah and Omaha, Canada had Gold, Britain had Juno and Sword. This area covered most of the Normandy coast, from Cotention east to Deauville.

This was a distance of fifty miles or more. At 6:30am, the Neptune battering-ram struck full force against this sector. At Utah beach, Laffey stood close to shore protecting minesweepers and landing craft. As this hurricane of steel hit the beach, it seemed as if the shoreline might be blown away. The hammer of guns and exploding shells, bombs, mines and machine guns was a constant roar. The sand and sea seemed to quake in unison. Through the smoke and dust and acrid fumes, the whirling sand and churning sea, American soldiers could be seen charging across the beach.

While Utah Beach exploded, churned, erupted and roared in agony, destroyer USS Corry DD463, dealing out salvo (artillery discharge) after salvo onto the beach, hit a mine at 6:33am. Though mortally wounded, Corry was trying desperately to bring her situation under control when German battery took her under fire. Corry sank under the barrage.

The landing area was growing as we pushed more troops and equipment ashore. The minesweepers had cleared a great area of mines, and Laffey could move more freely along the beachhead. The number of dead American soldiers in the water was increasing also. With the approach of darkness, Laffey withdrew from the beach to take up screening positions to the northwest of the transport area. The Germans maintained a huge torpedo boat base in Cherbourg. These boats would be out in force with the arrival of darkness. We had to keep them from beachhead. The night passed without the torpedo boats invading Laffey's screen. But, the German shells continued to fall and German planes continued to sow mines in the landing area.

D-Day plus one, June 7, 1944, found Laffey back on the firing line. Twenty-four hours had made a great change in the picture. The beachhead was expanding rapidly and targets for the big guns of the battleships and cruisers had been pushed inland out of reach of the Laffey's guns. But, there were plenty of targets in pockets of resistance that were in our range. Laffey went to work right away. With spotters on the ground and in the air, our fire was

very effective. Bombardment continued all that day and Laffey returned to the picket line for the night.

D-Day plus two, June 8, 1944, started in a somber note. At 1:53am, our sister ship Meredith DD726 hit a mine. She sank later with great loss of life. Destroyer Glennon DD620 hit a mine about 8:00am, ran aground and was finished off by shore batteries. Destroyer escort Rich DE695 was destroyed by more than one mine while trying to assist Glennon. Rich lost about ninety men. Laffey spent June 8th and 9th on the firing line expanding about seventy percent of our 5" ammunition. On June 9th, there was quite a hair-raising experience for me. In the early afternoon, we had retired from the firing line for a little break and fresh air. We were some five miles back from the firing line and, at that time, things were really quiet. I had a little break from my duty station and stepped out on the torpedo deck. I did this as often as I could to clear my head and catch a look at what went on out there. This time, I heard a plane approaching – a German plane. German planes gave off a different sound from their engines than U.S. planes. The German plane sound was like a misfire at the end of each firing cycle.

The crew of the Part 40 MM gun crew sat directly one deck below me. I yelled down to them in an attempt to let them know what I heard. They heard me and in turn attempted to get the attention of the officers on the bridge. At that moment, the plane entered my range of vision as it cleared the after stack. Then, I really began yelling at the crew below! It was a German bomber flying at about five hundred feet altitude. As I yelled "Get him! Get him, boys!," I saw and heard the bomb bay doors open. For some reason, the gunners never received permission to fire. No one fired. The plane continued on toward the beachhead area sowing his mines.

On June 10th, the Laffey requested, and was granted, permission to return to England for fuel and ammunition. At 2:30pm, we tied up to an oiler in Plymouth Harbor. The only excitement on the trip was dinging a floating aerial torpedo. Our 20 MM gun crews whetted their marksmanship in exploring the torpedo. One human interest story developed during this re-supply trip to Plymouth. After fueling, we moved to an ammunition supply ship. Normally, all hands turn-to in the loading of ammunition. As usual, I managed to find important work in the radio room. I noticed that in the line sweating under those five-inch projectiles were two British sailors. They looked to be sixteen or seventeen years old, and I wondered why they were working so hard on the Laffey. My unasked question was answered in the chow line.

I stayed holed-up until I heard the boatswain blow for chow-down (meal time). The two British sailors were just ahead of me in line. As the line snaked along the deck and down the hatch to the chow hall, I learned how blessed it is to be born in the United States. These men-boys were becoming more excited as we

approached the hatch. When they reached the ladder and could see into the mess hall, they really got excited. One grabbed the other and began actually to shake him, excitedly saying "I told you! See! I told you! They have it!" As I took a peek toward the direction he pointed in, I realized it was ice cream bars he referred to. I had to wipe a few tears away from my eyes. Here these two men-boys were fighting for their country and freedom, and they probably couldn't even remember eating ice cream. Those sailors had put in a hard day's work for an ice cream bar. I wasted no time in placing my bar on one tray and reached for an extra for the other tray. Before the reached their table, their trays were fairly loaded down with ice cream bars.

Laffey was a new class and a very modern ship for its time. We not only had an ice cream machine, but we also had fresh water evaporators that could supply the boilers and enough for showers also. This is something the older destroyer crews before us only dreamed of.

Early morning on June 12th found us back on station of Utah and Omaha Beaches. Our army was rapidly moving inland and most targets were beyond Laffey's guns. Battleships and cruisers were still hammering the Germans twenty-five to thirty miles away. These ships needed to be protected as German bombers, submarines and torpedo boats were plentiful. At 1:00am, Laffey's radar scope came alive with blips signaling the arrival of e-boats. At that moment, to the northwest was the USS Nelson DD 623 and to our east was USS Somers DD381, The Nelson turned her spotlight on the e-boats and opened fire. Laffey and the Somers followed suit and opened fire immediately. The e-boats split into three groups and changed course. The Nelson was immediately hit by a torpedo. Laffey and Somers gave chase. Somers made final contact in the next few minutes, then the chase fell to the Laffey. The sea foamed as Laffey reached for top speed and our five-inch guns made a terrible noise. Within a few miles the faster e-boats

The mess hall

were pulling out of range. Laffey was fast, but the e-boats were faster. We were forced to give up and the torpedo boat escaped. The Nelson was out of action and in tow to England.

The sea was not kind since the invasion began. Now, she seemed to attach with a vengeance. On June 16th, our best pier for off-loading heavy equipment and ammunition was destroyed by a storm. Our army advancing on the part of Cherbourg was slowed due to lack of artillery shells. The Germans were determined that we should not take the deep waters. We had to take to Cherbourg to keep our army supplied. Our naval guns had the ability to take the port. The orders came on June 20th: enter Cherbourg Harbor and destroy the German fortifications! The assault date was planned for June 25th, 1944.

At 9:25pm on June 21st, we headed for Portland, England, for fuel and ammunition. The Cotentin Peninsula juts into the English Channel at the northwestern most part of Normandy. The tip of the peninsula is u-shaped. The city of Cherbour lay at the base in the middle between two extended bulges of land, the one on the east being nearest Utah Beach. The heavy German batteries were located on a nine-mile strip on either side of Cherbourg and sighted to protect the city.

The bombardment ships were split into two groups. Group one was made up of the heavy cruisers Tuscaloosa and Quincy, Royal navy cruisers Glasgow and Enterprise, six American destroyers and the battleship USS Nevada. Group two consisted of the battleships USS Texas and USS Arkansas and the destroyers USS Barton, USS O'Brien USS Hobson, USS Plunkett and the Laffey. British and American minesweepers would clear the approaches and bombardment areas. Fighter planes of the U.S. 9th Army Air Force would cover us against the German air force. At 3:30am on June 25th, a Sunday, Laffey and the other bombardment ships steamed out of Portland Harbor, England, toward the two heavily fortified areas of Cherbourg with orders to reduce them to rubble.

The trip was uneventful, but there were no surprises. As soon as group one's minesweepers entered the bombardment area, they were spotted and batteries on shore opened fire on them. Then, the show began! HMS Glasgow and HMS Enterprise went to work on the battery. HMS Glasgow was hit twice. Finally, HMS Enterprise finished the job and the battery was silenced. Group two, following our minesweepers at five knots, entered the arc of Battery Hamburg's big 11 inch guns and all hell broke loose. There were other batteries – lots of them. And the closer to Cherbourg we got, the more there seemed to be.

O'Brien was sent to cover the minesweepers with gunfire and smoke. But O'Brien could not do the job alone. Barton and Laffey were sent to assist. Laffey took Battery Hamburg under fire, or, the spot where we thought it was located. The smoke and dust was so

heavy by this time that it was difficult to identify the target. Battery Hamburg turned its guns on the destroyers. What a frustrating and maddening situation. It was bad enough to be shot at, but not being able to see the shooter makes it worse.

Wham! Barton took a hit. "Right full rudder," our commanding officer yelled. "All engines ahead flank!"

Laffey leapt ahead at twenty-five knots zig-zagging, firing and making smoke. The big guns on the Texas bellowed, the big guns on the Arkansas bellowed, the shore batteries bellowed, and between the bellows were the constant bark of the five-inch guns on the destroyers and secondary batteries of the battleships. Laffey dodged, shot and created smoke for the battleships while at the same time fired at the gun flashes on shore.

Wham! A blast like that of some giant hand slaps the water off the port bow. No explosion. No flying chunks of steel. No staggering in the water. But Laffey is hit. A hole gaped in the port side and a huge projectile lay in the chain locker – a dud. The shell hit the water, skipped and hit Laffey just above the water line. We did not know o f the damage until after the fight when damage control had a chance to inspect the ship.

At about 12:53pm, O'Brien staggered. Laffey was just astern and some of her crew saw the explosions as a huge shell struck O'Brien's signal bridge. The CIC was out, the radar damaged and thirteen men were dead. The battleship Texas took a hit on the navigation bridge. Shortly thereafter, Texas scored with a hit on one of the Battery Hamburg's guns. Then, at 3:01pm, Laffey and group two were ordered to return to England. The army was overrunning the city of Cherbourg. We could not fire without endangering the lives of our own troops. Our work at Cherbourg was finished. By early July, allied troops, guns and war supplies were pouring into France through the port at Cherbourg.

Laffey stopped in Portland, England, long enough to patch the shell hole in the port bow. We finally reached Belfast, Northern Ireland, on June 30th. At 7:00a, on July 3rd, we cleared Belfast Harbor bound for Boston, Massachusetts, USA. The trip was uneventful except for a little rough weather. Most of the crew could take rough seas in stride. We were old salts by this time. Of course, to Laffey herself, rough seas were a stroll in the park. She pitched and rolled under two waves and over on. One minute the bow was thirty feet above the water, and the next minute the screws were high out of the water and spinning like mad. After each ducking, Laffey would shake off the foam much like a proud swan taking a leisurely swim.

We arrived in Boston Harbor in early afternoon on July 9th. A ten-day leave was coming up but I was a long way from home. Four of my ten days were spent traveling. About all I did was to change the type of transportation. It was wonderful to go home, but I just didn't have time to see everyone or get anything done.

Laffey sailed from Boston in early August of 1944 after repairs, renovations and instillation of some new equipment. We also put in more practice, steaming and did calibration of radar equipment. With that completed, we sailed from Norfolk, Virginia, for the Panama Canal on August 26th. The trip through the Panama Canal was very exciting to me. From the Caribbean Sea, you enter the canal and are lifted to the top of a mountain by a series of locks. At the top is a huge lake with canals joining other lakes and ten returned to sea level on the west by more locks. Once we made it through, we sailed on to San Diego, California, for supplies. We then arrived in Pearl Harbor in the Hawaiian Islands on September 18th, 1944. While there, we put in more training in the waters around Hawaii. Our gunners were good on surface and shore targets. But, their shooting at aircraft needed some polishing. The western Pacific area was full of Japanese planes, and the pilots were showing signs of becoming suicidal, sacrificing their lives with plane and bomb for their cause.

Shortly, in company with other destroyers and the battleship North Carolina, the Laffey sailed enroute to Eniwetok Atoll in the Marshall Islands. The U.S. had been pushing the Japanese relentlessly, and there was no time for a letup. Something big was being planned. Either the Philippines or Farmosa would probably be the next target. We didn't have long to wait before radio traffic informed us that General McArthur had returned to the Philippines. Even at that time, battleships West Virginia, Mississippi and Maryland screened by destroyers were pounding the east coast of Leyte Island with their big guns from stations in Leyte Gulf. The army was landing on Leyte in the central Philippines. There was just a little touch of regret they had started without Laffey. But, we would catch up. Leyte was a key Japanese stronghold in the defense of the Philippines, and McArthur had touched a raw nerve in the Japanese war machine. There would be a fight – a long fight – and there would be plenty for Laffey when she got there.

There was a swift reaction, a violent reaction, as the Japanese committed their fleet in a do-or-die effort to save the Philippines. The bottoms of these seas were already crowded with sunken American, British and Japanese ships left there when prior sea battles raged across these waters in 1942. More would be stacked upon them in the next few weeks. The Japanese rushed reinforcements from their home islands. They split into two forces for a pincers movement on our forces at Leyte. One force was to move through the Surigas Straights and join another force coming south along the east coast of Samar. A good plan if it worked.

However, it didn't work. As Admiral Shoji Nishimura's southern forces entered the waters off norhten Mindanao, they were attacked and mauled by American aircraft. A part of the fleet was put out of action by the planes. But, the bulk ran head-on into the ghost of Pearl Harbor. Rear Admiral Jesse B. Oldendorf's battle-line was crossing the eastern entrance to Surigas Straight.

Admiral Nishimura was in bad trouble. Oldendorf had crossed the Japenese T. This meant that the American ships could fire broadside salvos (a simultaneous discharge of artillery or other guns in a battle) at the Japanese ships while the Japanese could only return fire with their forward turrets.

American battleships West Virginia, Mississippi, California, Maryland, Tennessee and Pennsylvania, all victims of the December 7, 1941 attack on Pearl Harbor, exacted terrible revenge. American destroyers and PT boats added insult to injury as they attacked from part and starboard. The southern force of the Japanese fleet was unmercifully pummeled. The Japanese eastern fleet steaming south along the east coast of Samar had been hit on October 24th by American planes and suffered heavy losses including the battleship Musashi that was sister ship to the mighty Yamato battleship. This still-mighty force was heading into more trouble as it ran into a force of American escort carriers and screen of destroyers and destroyer escorts on October 25th. The battle that followed is a book of its own.

Vice Admiral Kurita's force spotted the Americans. At the same time, the American spotter pilot alerted Admiral Sprague that the Japanese were approaching. Four of their battleships, Kongo, Nagato, Haruna and Yamato, seven cruisers and eleven destroyers were coming from the north and closing in at thirty knots. Admiral Sprague questioned the spotter pilot as to the identity of the ships. The pilot answered that they had Pagoda masts and looked like Japanese to him.

The Japanese opened fire at seventeen miles. Sprague screamed for help on his radio, ordered full speed into the wind and launched every air plane available. Destroyers, destroyer escorts and body flat-tops were never expected to stand and slug it out with battleships, and certainly not the super-battleship Yamato. But stand they did, and slug it out they did. The only immediate help was another escort carrier group commanded by Rear Admiral F.B. Stump some fifty miles south of Admiral Sprague's group. Halsey's third fleet was far to the north. Oldendorf's force in Leyte

Gulf was low on fuel and ammunition and re-grouping from the Surigas battle. Admiral Sprague found himself and Rear Admiral Stump's group the only Americans between Kurita's mighty battleships and the Leyte landing sight. They must keep those battleships away from the beachhead and American transports at any cost.

First to attach the Japanese heavyweights was the USS Johnston. At 7:20am, Johnston peeled away and hurled a full torpedo spread at a Japanese cruiser. Immediately, Johnston received a cyclone of Japanese shells. She reeled through the water with her speed reduced to seventeen knots. Taking hit after hit, she kept up a hot fire on the cruisers at ranges as close as five thousand yards.

The five inch guns of destroyers and destroyer escorts were no match for the six, eight, fourteen, sixteen and eighteen inch guns of the Japanese cruisers and battleships. Yet, the "small boys" never hesitated. USS Hoel rushed a battleship with half a salvo of torpedoes and was hammered by shells. Hoel managed to get off another half salvo of torpedoes that damaged a heavy cruiser. Destroyer Heermann flung seven torpedoes at a cruiser, and six minutes later she released three more at a battleship. Then, bold as brass, Heermann exchanged gun fire with two heavy cruisers. Luckey Heermann! With tons of shells falling around her, she was only slightly damaged. The destroyer escorts were all over the sea launching torpedoes, raking the superstructure of cruisers and battleships with their five inch guns. Roberts, Dennis, Butler and Raymond all did their jobs and took a beating. The Japanese were slowed until reinforcements could arrive, but not without a price. Carrier escort Gambier Bay was sunk. Destroyers Hoel, Hermann and Johnston were sunk. Destroyer escort Roberts was sunk. As the Japanese withdrew to the north, Halsey's third fleet planes caught them in the North Philippines Sea. Most were scared by bomb hits before they escaped.

Laffey was assigned to Task Force 38.4 on November 5, 1944. The fight for Leyte was far fro over, and our job was to pound Japanese positions any place in the Philippines we could find them. This was a full-time job. Here, Laffey was introduced to the Japanese suicide planes known as kamikazes.

By mid-November, Laffey was back in the Ulithi Atoll for a new assignment. Ulithi at that time was our westernmost forward operations base. The lagoon was large enough and deep enough to accommodate all types of ships. With seven hundred spaces for capital ships plus numerous small craft buzzing around like a swarm of bees, the anchorage resembled a huge shopping center parking lot at rush hour. This was a perfect staging area located in the Western Caroline Islands group with good barrier reefs. Yet, it was not perfectly safe. Only a few hours before we arrived, a suicide plane had crashed and sunk one of our large oil tankers in the anchorage. Two kamikazes must have followed us because a night or two after arrival, they attacked. We were enjoying a smoker (a play) on the forecastle (the forward part of the ship below deck). The smoker was a comedy show performed by numbers of the crew. This was a real interesting performance. But, about half-way through, two Japanese kamikazes came barreling over the lagoon. One crashed into a carrier just before reaching us, and the other roared directly over us at about one hundred feet altitude and, I suppose, thinking he had a large aircraft carrier in his sights, plunged into the tiny island of Mog Mog. That pilot must have had a depressing surprise. There was nothing on Mog Mog except a couple of wrecked landing barges, a small pier, the twisted carcass of a British scout plane and debris from our day-before recreational party. All the palm and coconut trees had been knocked off earlier. That really put out our smoker, and it was a good one.

Laffey was attached to Admiral Kinkaid's seventh fleet. We departed Ulithi on November 27 not sure of where we were going but we made a good guess. The army on Leyte was behind schedule, not doing too well because of bad weather, lack of landing strips for fighters and the constant troop reinforcements by the Japanese through Ormoc Bay. There must be another landing on Leyte's west side. Leyte is about one hundred miles long north to south and twenty to forty miles wide. A mountain range splits the island from north to south. The southern part is low and marshy during wet season. This just happened to be the wet season. Laffey entered Leyte Gulf on November 29, 1944. A quick look around the beachhead anchorage was enough to tell us all we needed to know. We were at Leyte. Kincaid's seventh fleet was used to put troops ashore and keep them there. The landing craft were assembled. Very soon we would land them in the Ormoc Bay.

Before this landing force was ready to sail, there was some activity, comical and otherwise. Coxswain Pressburger (a coxswain is the steersman of a ship's boat) was ordered to run Dr. Darnell by boat over to the hospital ship Hope. While waiting for the doctor to finish his business, Pressburger was directed to a barge near the beach to remove some doctors and deliver them to the Hope. Pressburger found the barge to be about four feet higher than his boat. Fearing someone might be hurt or even break a leg making the jump from the barge to his boat, the coxswain, a husky strong man, offered to catch each one under their arms as they jumped to help them make a safe landing. The light was not very good, but the plan was working until the last doctor jumped from the barge. Pressburger reached up, grabbing for a good hold. But, the jumper landed a little off-balance and staggered. The coxswain hugged tightly then froze that way until a very manly voice coming from the facility of his arms said "You can let me go when ready, honey." Pressburger automatically released him.

The next night, our commanding officer, F.J. Beckton, scame on the intercom and told the crew that he had some news that he wanted us to be informed of. We were going into Ormoc Bay to test the Japanses defenses. He said that it was that the Japanese had placed submarines, suicide planes, surface ships and mines in the bay. "Other than that," he said, "you don't have a damned thing to worry about." Captain Beckton was strictly Navy and well-liked and respected by his crew. The way to check the defenses is to go into the bay and prowl around while the shore batteries fire at you.

Pin-point the gun positions, knock out what you can and zig-zag like hell for leather out there. Laffey was lucky we made it out. Destoyer Cooper was not so lucky. She still sits on the bottom of the Ormoc Bay.

At 11:30am, December 6th, Laffey steamed south on the east side of Leyte Island as a part of Admiral A.D. Struble's Ormoc assault force. Our mission was to take the army's 77 Division around the southern tip of Leyte, back up into Ormoc Bay and land them on two beaches below the town of Ormoc. We were to help take pressure off the other units and battle the Japanese army in the southern part of Leyte, take port of Ormoc and strangle the enemy. That sounded simple enough.

At 6:30am on December 7, 1944, the Laffey was stationed off the beaches on the eastern side of Ormoc Bay. Most of the Japanese troops were to the south fighting the oncoming American 7th Division. We were landing behind them. Yet, it would be no cake walk. There were gun emplacements and, as our rocket launching LSM's launched their barrages, those guns let go. The battery's shells came in with a woosh-boom-woosh raising waterspouts, straddling Laffey too close. Laffey opened fire. The bombardment was on. The invasion was on. The kamikazes were on.

Here they came! It seemed the skies opened up, and down came the divine wind on all of us. It didn't bother the army so much, but it sure played hell with our ships. Laffey was in the northern part of the bay. Other well-armed ships were in bombarding positions along the eastern beaches. The Japanese came from the northwest. This meant that the minesweepers, picket ships, empty transports and other ships having moved away from the beaches bore the brunt of the attack. We had both army and air force cover, but because of bad flying conditions, they just could not get out enough planes into the air to do much good.

USS Mahan, on picket duty fifteen miles to the southwest, was the first to be hit. Three direct hits by kamikazes were too much. After a losing battle with fire and explosions, she was abandoned. USS Walke sent Mahan to the bottom with torpedo and gunfire. Ward, a fast transport, was next to be hit. A suicide plane struck her port side amidships. With no hope of saving her, USS O'Brien was ordered to sink Ward with gunfire.

The attacks continued. Laffey beat off two attacks. At about 1:00pm, Admiral Struble ordered the task force to withdraw. We had done what we came to do. The army's 77th Division was ashore and the empty landing ships were no longer needed. As we withdrew to the south, the Japanese followed. Destroyer escort Liddle was hit. USS Lamson was also hit. USS Flusser covered Lamson and both ships were saved but expended all ammunition in doing so. USS Barton fought off an attack. The kamikazes kept after us until about 6:40pm. It was then too dark for them to see us, and we were well on our way back to the Leyte anchorage on the east side of the island.

The Rising Sun was setting. We knew it, and the Japanese knew it too. But, they would desperately fight on – we knew that too. The Japanese Navy was no longer a threat, but the kamikaze remained a problem. Kamikaze means "divine wind", and the Japanese used the term to identify their suicide pilots. It seems that sometime in the thirteenth century, the Mongolians set sail from the mainland to invade Japan. But, before they reached the islands, a typhoon roared down on the Japan Sea and destroyed the would-be invaders. The Japanese believed that their Diving Wind, or suicide pilots, could yet prevail against the American Navy and sweep us from the western Pacific Ocean in the same way as that typhoon swept away the invaders all those centuries ago. So, they adopted that name "kamikaze." Everything now depended on the suicidal acts of those pilots. Enough kamikazes could kill any ship. We knew that now. From here on out, it would be us against the Divine Wind blowing from Japan.

December 10, 1994, found Laffey well at sea screening cruisers Boise and Phoenix. Even after Ormoc Bay, the morale among the Laffey crew was good. We had seen a lot of carnage, a little of what some would call hell on earth. It seemed that with each encounter and each conflict, the carnage was a little worse. But, we believed Laffey would survive. Our gunners were the best. Our communications division was second to none. We could take and we could dish it out, but we believed we could dish out more than we would ever have to take. The men trusted the officers, and the officers trusted the men.

Before December 10, the stamina and morale of this crew would be tested once again as we would view the destruction inflicted by yet another kamikaze on a ship at sea. USS Hughes was on picket duty near Surigas Straight and Dinagat Island when attacked by Japanese planes. Not all of those planes were suicidal. Some made runs, dropped bombs and pulled out. But, one did not release his bomb nor pull out. The Hughes' gunners pounded him, but he kept coming. He crashed amidships and exploded on impact. The engine and boiler rooms were ripped open and Hughes was helpless in the water. The Japanese planes moved on, apparently believing the Hughes was finished. But, Hughes was not finished and her call for help was heard. Laffey was pulled away from the screening assignment and sent racing to aid the Hughes. Meanwhile, high winds were driving Hughes toward the beach.

Darkness had fallen when Laffey arrived on the scene. We viewed the damage by floodlight. The kamikaze has hit amidships just above the waterline and exploded. The hole was large enough to accommodate a freight car. Our crew immediately turned to help transfer the wounded to Laffey's sick bay and rig towing gear. With not much time to spare, Laffey took up slack in the tow line and began to move her away from the dangerous shoreline and toward Leyte anchorage. Hughes suffered eighteen dead and twenty badly injured. Laffey's crew gazed at the gaping hole, the

The Captain's quarters

dead and injured and, no doubt, many wondered how long it would be until our ship would look like that.

On the afternoon of December 11, Hughes was in port, the wounded off-loaded and Laffey was ready for more steaming. The wait was not long because San Pedro anchorage was filled with all typed of ships and more were arriving by the hour. The next day, December 12, we became a part of a huge task group preparing to put troops ashore on Mindoro. Mindoro was important to us because of its dry climate. Located about one-hundred-and-fifty miles west of the southern tip of Luzon, Mindoro was to be a vital stepping stone to the liberation of the Philippines. We needed land-based air cover, and Mindoro, with less rainfall than Leyte, offered the chance for better air strips. Besides, it was much closer to the target.

Deception played a key role in the Mindoro operation. From San Pedro, Laffey steamed south with a task force through Leyte Gulf to confuse the reconnaissance pilots. As darkness fell, we headed west through the Surigas Straights into the Mindanao Sea. Ahead of us was another force including escort carriers, battleships, cruisers and destroyers. This first force was to head west around the southern tip of Negros, continue on a westward course into the Sulu Sea and make a feint (which means deceptive movement) at Palawan. Palawan was a long slender island about two hundred miles southwest of Mindoro and an important Japanese base. We wanted to deceive the enemy into believing we were headed there. The ruse worked. When we reached Negros with the transports and landing craft sometime later, the enemy realized we were turning north and began to react.

At about 3:00 pm on December 13, Laffey was steaming on station about five hundred yards to port of the light cruiser Nashville. At the time, our radar was pretty well blinded by the high mountains as we steamed through the narrow straights. All of a sudden, the kamikaze roars over the mountain top and across Laffey's bow with his eye on the Nashville. Wham! He hit just below the bridge of Nashville on the port side. He was aiming for the bridge, but he did alright. Nashville was Admiral Arthur Struble's flagship, and she was loaded with extra officers and enlisted men. Many were killed outright.

No one had time to fire at the first plane, but we were ready for the second one, and he wasn't long in coming. Laffey was trying to get alongside the Nashville to assist, but exploding ammunition aboard Nashville and the approach of the second kamikaze made the task difficult. The kamikaze received most of the Laffey's attention. The accurate shooting by Laffey's gunners made the suicider's position untenable. He went back across the mountain about as fast as he had come. The Nashville was forced to return to San Pedro, Leyte, for repairs.

December 14 was mostly uneventful as the invasion force steamed steadily on toward Mindoro. We had the enemy on the run

The bridge

and there was no intention of letting them rest. The war was far from over. We needed to take the Philippines as quick as possible and push on toward Japan. We needed Mindoro, and on December 15, 1944, we took it.

Mindoro was lightly defended. Evidently, the Japanese considered it unimportant to their defense of the Philippine Islands. The bombardment and landings met little resistance, and by noon, San Jose, the only town of any size on the island, was securely in American hands. But, the kamikaze kept right on coming from the skies. The pilots were getting smarter all the time. There were as many small islands with high hills close to the beach. The pilots would fly low behind the hills until they could line up their targets, then over the hill the plunged with throttle open. Wham! Another landing ship would be scattered across the beach. Luckily for us, the planes were a little late and most of the landing craft on the beachheads were empty.

Our fighter planes did a wonderful job in helping to break up these suicide attacks, but there were just too many for our fighters and naval guns to get them all. The best thing we could do was to get our landing craft onto the beach, unload and pull them out as soon as possible. Within hours after the initial landing, Laffey left Mindoro with thirty-one landing craft tanks and twelve landing ship medium. With us also was the landing craft commander in the fast transport Lloyd and destroyers Hopewell and Pringle. Some carrier-based fighters were overhead as cover. We left much better.

We had no trouble until about 4:40 pm on December 16. A bogey appeared on our radar screen. He was out of range of our guns and seemed to be a little shy about coming closer. We vectored some fighter planes in on him. About six minutes later, one of the fighter pilots in a calm voice announced over his radio "Tally ho." The Japanese had one less plane and pilot. A few days later, we safely reached San Pedro anchorage.

On Christmsa Day of 1944, Laffey finally was able to enjoy a day of rest and a good dinner. We had both bad and good luck. Bad luck had come back on Thanksgiving when we had to leave our Thanksgiving dinner on the supply ship and go chasing north with the fast aircraft carriers. The good came here at Christmas. The supply ship had not forgotten us. They had kept our Thanksgiving dinner. Now, we had Thanksgiving and Christmas at the same time. What a dinner!

Destroyers are the work horses of the Navy. When I thought we had done everything a ship could do, there was something else that I had not though about. We had settled down to let our stomachs enjoy that good dinner, then we got orders along with Destroyer Walke to hoist anchor and pull alongside heavy cruiser Louisville anchored a short distance away. Laffey tied up on one side and Walke on the other. Before I really realized what was happening, the cruise had sucked our fuel tanks dry. We had just enough fuel left to get back to the oiler. Of course, it was much

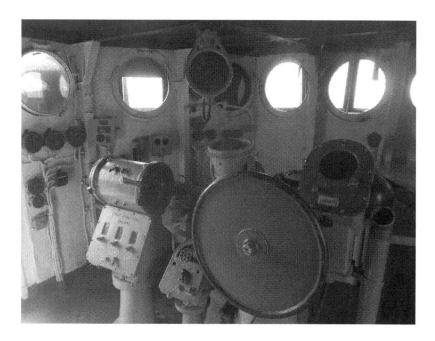

easier and faster for us to take fuel to the large cruiser than for her to come in to the oiler. There was a reason for this that we didn't know at that time. Louisville needed a full supply of fuel in the case her big guns were needed – and they were most definitely needed.

Laffey had reached the stationary oiler at about dusk, and about the time we finished filling our tanks, the flash radio report cam. The Japanese were out in force and headed toward the Mindoro beachhead. Cruisers Louisville, Phoenix, Boise and Minneapolis, with a screen of destroyers, were already in motion. The next radio message was for Laffey to chase after them. It would be another long night.

The Japanese had apparently decided to make one last effort to dislodge the Americans from Mindoro. They were unable to reinforce their garrison because of lack of ships and the ability to mount an invasion force. The Japanese Navy was ordered to destroy the beachhead. Rear Admiral Kimura, with a force of one heavy cruiser, one light cruiser and seven destroyers, sailed from Camrahn Bay (in what is now Vietnam) on December 24th en route to Mindoro. Bad weather concealed the force until about 4:00 pm on December 26 when it was sighted by a Navy patrol plane. By this time, the task force was some two hundred miles west of Mindoro in the South China Sea.

The patrol plane could not get a clear look at the Japanese fleet because of the weather. They had the number of ships and their course accurate, but could not identify it properly. The report was that the heavy cruiser was thought to be the battleship Yamato. This added a little excitement to our mission. The Yamato was the largest battleship in the world weighing in at sixty-three-thousand tons. Laffey's turn screws dug in as her speed increased. The bow wave peeled away in a beautiful, long foaming line on either side, and her wake boiled and stretched out for miles as she churned the sea in pursuit of Rear Admiral J.E. Chandler's task group.

It seemed to be an endless chase, but at 6:00 am we had caught up to Chandler, occupied our assigned position in the formation and pressed on toward Mindero. We arrived off the beachhead early in the afternoon, but we were too late. Admiral Rimura had beaten us. The admiral must have known we were coming. He lobbed a few shells into San Jose, inflicting very little damage. He dropped a few more shells along the coast and then disappeared. This was Japan's last real organized naval effort. After this, their main attacks came by way of the Divine Wind.

December 30th found Laffey back at San Pedro anchorage, refueled and ready for the next assignment. We had lots of company. The place was filled with ships and more kept coming. Something big was brewing. We knew that the main island of Luzon was next. For some reason the Japanese chose to ignore our concentration of ships at San Pedro. Surely they knew we were there. They also knew we would be heading north in a short time, so maybe their thinking was to let us get a little closer. They finally

The Captain's chair

did check us out about midnight on December 31st by way of one lone bogey. All he did was cause a mighty scramble to battle stations.

On January 2nd, 1945, Laffey along with one-hundred and sixty-three other ships under the command of Vice Admiral J.B. Oldendorf set sail from San Pedro en route to the beaches of Lingayear Gulf on the west side of Luzon some one hundred miles north of Manila. This was quite a jump for an invasion force of such size – seven hundred miles or more. Our job was cut out for us: fight the Divine Wind all the way, soften up the beaches, put the army ashore, protect the supply line and continue to fight the Divine Wind. The Japanese General Yamashita knew he could not hold the Philippines. There would be no reinforcements for him. He wanted to delay our forces on the beach long enough for the kamikazes to work on our ships.

Destroyer squadron Sixty, Laffey, O'Brien, Allen M. Sumner, Walke, Lowry, Ingraham, Moale and Barton sailed as party of the protective screen for the heavy bombardment ships. The protective screen protects the battleships and cruisers who are giving the attention to the shore targets. The destroyers also take their turn working the beach over when there are short-range targets. With us were the battleships Pennsylvania, California, New Mexico, West Virginia and also heavy cruisers Louisville, Minneapolis, HMAS Australia and HMAS Shropshire. In our group were six escort carriers, some fast transports and just about every other kind of ships except the fast battleships and large carriers. These were in the fast cruiser task groups of the third fleet.

This was a huge formation as we passed through the Surigao Straights headed west into the Sulu Sea. We were stretched out for miles. From Laffey's position, it was stretched from horizon to horizon. Fore and aft, we could not see the end. Surely, the Japanese could not fail to spot this huge assembly. But, for thirty-six hours no ship in our part of the formation was attacked. Suddenly, on the evening of January 3rd, a lone suicider appeared out of the sky and headed for the Australian cruiser Shropshire, Then, the sky began to blossom with puffs of smoke from exploding five inch shells as tracers from AA guns wove patterns among them. This spoiled the aim of the Japanese and he missed the cruiser. His watery grave was marked by a huge explosion and waterspout as the bomb hailed tons and tons of water into the air.

We knew that this lone pilot had radioed our position back to his base, but about twenty-four hours had passed before another plane appeared. We had more than three-hundred miles of steaming ahead of us, and much of it would be less than one-hundred miles from Japanese airbases on Luzon. We were close enough now. We must pass, and they must try to stop us. Laffey was like an outsider, a floating gun platform. We had to protect the convoy of troops and supplies. Sure, we had help. There were many gun platforms, but when they came at our section, it was Laffey against the kamikazes.

On January 4th at about 5:45 pm, the next attack occurred. Again, a lone plane approached. I don't know how he got past out combat air patrol, but someone on the talk between ships was screaming that a bogey was diving on a part of our formation. This time, the intended victim was the carrier escort Lunga Point. Good shooting by the escorts and good maneuvering by the Lunga Point caused this one to miss as well. Another huge explosion and waterspout followed.

This proved to be a good start, but only the start, for the fight was on. We shifted, turned, twisted and changed course, for they were coming! The next kamikaze came in a roaring power-dive straight for the 7,800 ton carrier escort Ommaney Bay. She could not dodge. The Japanese plane bounced off the superstructure onto the flight deck, but the bombs kept going and exploded deep within the ship. The flames turned her plated white-hot and her ammunition began to explode. The order to abandon ship was given at 8:00 pm. Destroyer Burns was ordered to torpedo the carrier. Ommaney Bay sank in the Sula Sea about fifty miles south of the Mindoro Straights. We steamed on through the straights that

night without incident. On January 5th, we reached the South China Sea west of Luzon, and the free ride was over. It was only a short flight from airfields on Luzon like Clark, Nelson and Nicholas. The Japanese took off in droves.

    A bogey appeared on Laffey's radar about daybreak. He would move in and back off, then come in again. This kept up for an hour, and finally he came into range. Laffey opened fire and O'Brien joined in. Together, they brought the bogey down just off O'Brien's bow. Things however would get worse. Destroyer escort Stafford was hit and put out of action. The cruiser Australia took a bad hit. Carrier escort Manila Bay took a blow on the flight deck. The Australian destroyer Arunta was attacked but the Japanese missed. Heavy cruiser Louisville was hit in the number two mount. This had not been a good day. We were still twelve hours from Lingayen Gulf.

Early the next morning, January 6th, 1945, we reached the entrance to Lingayen Gulf. Here, we began to form in groups. Minesweepers, bombardment groups, screening groups and landing ships grouped together. Laffey took her station in the screen. We expected the short batteries to open up on the minesweepers at once. But, they did not. This was a little upsetting. The Japanese seemed to have changed their defensive tactics. Then, we realized there was no organized mine fields – just a few floaters. Therefore, the minesweepers were not a threat to the defense. The batteries were simply holding their fire to conceal their positions. Not one battery fired at the minesweepers. The Japanese aerial defense also held back. For three or four hours, the only planes in the air were American. But, that all changed late in the morning. A flight of ten kamikazes showed up.

Our combat air patrol planes splashed five and chased the other five out of the gulf. The CAP was doing a good job of keeping the Japanese planes away from the beachhead area. But, they could not get them all. At noon, a Japanese plane broke through and dived on the battleship New Mexico. Laffey and the other ships of the screen did our best to stop it. We hit him, and hit him again. He turned into a fireball, like a comet, but he kept coming. The kamikaze crashed into the port side of New Mexico's bridge and exploded in a shower of flaming gasoline and metal. About thirty sailors were killed. Laffey escorted the New Mexico clear of the crowded beachhead area even as another suicider tried to get his talons into her. We were ready for this one and shot hit down. New Mexico's crew brought the fires under control and returned to her task of shelling the beach in short order.

The kamikaze must have had some kind of grudge against our destroyer squadron. At 12:02 pm, a suicider plunged into Allen M. Sumner. Twelve men were killed, the superstructure was wrecked and one torpedo mount smashed. At 12:26 pm, the Lowry became badly damaged when a downed plane crashed into the sea nearby. At 12:40pm, our good buddy Walke really got it. Her gunners knocked out two kamikazes, but the third one ripped deep into her bridge and pilot house. Fire immediately enveloped the wreckage. The fourth plane came in and was shot down by Walke's gunners. O'Brien took a hit on the fantail and had to withdraw.

Many sailors were being killed in these attacks. The crashing planes, exploding bombs and flames that followed took their toll. Many other ships were being attacked. Light cruiser Columbia took a hit on the port side aft. She lost power and was forced to flood her magazines. Minesweeper Long was hit by two kamikazes and sank. Southard was hit in a fire room. Battleship California was hit in the after fire control director and flaming gasoline spread across her decks. HMAS Australia, which had already been hit the day before, took another hit. She also took three more hits during the Lingayen Gulf Operation. Louisville, also hit the day

before, was once again attacked. Louisville's gunners shot down two kamikazes but two more crashed aboard. The ship took a beating.

January 6, 1945, was a bad day. I had begun to wonder who was winning this war. In many cases, the Japanese were losing one plane and one pilot. In turn, the Americans were losing one ship and thirty to fifty sailors. Something just didn't add up right. The overall picture was a little better. The Japanese lost most of their Navy, Army and Air Force. A short three years earlier, the Japanese had landed on these same beaches to drive the Americans from the Philippines. Now, the tables were turned.

We needed more air cover. This would indeed help but still would not stop all of the kamikazes. Our fast cruiser task forces were ranging north and west, bombing enemy airfields on their home grounds. Our task group commander Admiral Oldendorf contacted Admiral Kinkaid for help. Kinkaid pulled the group back to join the group bombing Formosa, and by January 7th, those planes were pounding the air fields on Luzon. Things would be a little better today.

Early on January 7th, the Laffey, all that remained of destroyer squadron sixty and the other bombardment ships moved back in to position off the Lingayen beaches. This time, only a few suiciders appeared. Aircraft from our fast cruiser groups had done their job well. The minesweeper Palmer (DMS 5) was hit. A DMS was basically an older destroyer converted to a minesweeper. Some of these ships mounted five inch guns and, to the Japanese pilots, they were large warships, or regular destroyers.

Lingayen Gulf is u-shaped, thirty to forty miles long and about twenty-five miles wide. On January 7th, our targets were at the base of the "u" on and behind the beach. The town of Lingayen is located on the base of the "u" on the west side. The land here is low and swampy. The terrain and sunken ships were our problem. It was difficult to spot the targets on the low land and the sunken hulks were a menace to navigation. We were able to use some of the ship masts that were sticking out of the water as reference points to find some targets. In the late afternoon, we began to move our barrage inland to give the frogmen (underwater demolition teams) room to work. We expected all kinds of obstacles, explosive charges, mines and anything that could interrupt the landing of troops and materials. But, the frogmen found only a few mines. This was a surprise. Usually, you try to stop an invasion at the beach.

January 8th was practically a re-run of the 7th. A few kamikazes and few regular aircraft made attacks on our ships in the gulf. The cruiser Australia was hit two times. These were hits three and four for the Aussie since the operation began. These hits did little damage and the gallant ship kept right on firing. The Australian ship was a large high-structured vessel and, from the air, must have looked much like a troop transport. That would be the reason for the Japanese' interest in her.

Our attack transports, loaded with troops and equipment, were approaching the rendezvous at Lingayen Gulf with our bombardment group. These transports, Task Force 78 under Vice Admiral D.E. Barbay, and Task Force 79 under Vice Admiral T.S. Wilkinson, had followed the same route to Lingayen as we had taken. They had to run the same gauntlet of kamikaze attacks. But, there must have been fewer planes now. Ships had been hit. There had been casualties. Laffey and the other ships of Admiral Oldendorf's bombardment force were the lightning rod, and we really had drawn the kamikazes.

On January 9th, 1945, the amphibious troops went ashore. The landing was a success. We had pounded the Japanese' positions for four days with everything from fourteen inch shells to launches of specially equipped LCI rockets. The few Japanese left gave our troops little trouble. The stiffest opposition was on the easternmost flank near the village of Mabilo. The village was backed by the Zambales Mountains, and some of the Japanese were pretty well dug-in along those hills. It took a little urging from our bombs and naval guns to move them out. Our troops continued to advance. Before the day was over, it was very obvious that the troops would not need the Navy's baseball bat much longer. Running south from the beaches of Lingayen Gulf is a wide bush valley lying between two rugged jungle-covered mountain ranges all the way to Manila Bay, a classic invasion route that the Japanese knew very well. The Americans were lining up for a drive down this valley.

Troops ashore were doing well, but ships at sea were accumulating more problems. The night of January 9th brought out the first suicide boats in the gulf. These boats were a serious threat to our transports and smaller craft in the shallow waters near the beach. They carried a heavy depth charge in the bow. The charge could be released near a moored ship and set to explode in shallow water. Some damage was inflicted on a few ships, but the

destroyers could spot these boats and bow them out of the waters with their twenty and forty millimeter guns.

Another seagoing threat to our ships was the swimming kamikazes. These men would strap explosive charges to their bodies then conceal themselves under ponchos, wood crates or most anything that would float and slowly swim toward their intended target. Immediately, Laffey issued M-1 rifles to a few crewmen and told them to get some target practice. Some ponchos sank after one hit, and some wood crated changed course. Other ships were using this method to defend themselves. We had no idea of the number of kamikazes that were sent to the bottom in this way.

Laffey remained in Lingayen Gulf providing anti-submarine and anti-aircraft screen for the larger bombardment ships. We were aware that General McArthur's troops were doing right well. They needed little help from us. On our right, the western flank, our troops that had landed near Lingayen, were more than thirty miles south and pushing out of range of even our fourteen inch guns aboard the battleships. Troops had passed Malasiqui fifteen miles inland in the center and were depending on their own artillery and air cover. Troops on the left, or eastern flank, were having a little trouble with the enemy at Baguio well inland. There, they called on the Navy for gunfire. By January 16th, we had removed these fortified positions with gunfire, and the G.I.s increased speed toward Manila. Supply convoys were reaching the beaches and this was enough. Some of the battered ships of the heavy bombardment group were released by General McArthur. And with them, Laffey headed for Ulithi anchorage in the Caroline Islands.

On the afternoon of January 27th, what was left of Destroyer Squadron Sixty – Laffey, Barton, Moale and Ingraham – arrived in Ulithi lagoon anchorage escorting the battleships West Virginia and California. The anchorage was crowded with ships just as it was the last time we were there. Much more had happened in this location during our absence. Not only had the shore facilities been greatly developed, but a real base had sprung up. There were now facilities for repairing and overhauling ships, making it a complete instant major base built from scratch and which made our advance possible.

Due to the Laffey's ability to maneuver and the accuracy of her gunners, we had escaped battle damage. But we did need a check-up and minor repairs. Steaming thousands of miles, some of them at high speeds and great stress, can take its toll on a ship. Although the crew was working on the ship continually, maintaining, painting and repairing, there were some things they could not do at sea. Machinery wears out, and even barnacles grow on the hull below the waterline.

Laffey pulled alongside the destroyer tender Piedmont (AD 17) and requested a diver to go down and check the bottom. We needed extensive repairs to the rudders, a complete scraping of the hull, and a fresh coat of antifouling paint below the waterline. This work required time in dry dock. Before, this would have required a time-consuming trip to Pearl Harbor in Hawaii, but not now. Bases like Ulithi had their own dry docks. They were not on land, nor were they permanent installations. They were mobile. Dock landing ships were self-propelled. These vessels could steam forward when new bases were established as we advanced ever closer to Japan. Laffey was scheduled to enter a dry dock as soon as possible and, while the welders worked on the rudders, the crew would scrape off the barnacles and seaweed then paint the hull.

A floating dry dock is like a triangular box with open top and watertight gate at the stern. As Laffey moved up to the stern, the gate was opened and ballast tanks on each side were flooded until the bottom of the box sank to a point just below Laffey's bottom. With the gate open, the box, or interior of the dry dock, was flooded. Laffey moved inside, and the gate was closed and the water pumped out. The ballast tanks were pumped and filled with air. Laffey settled in the wooden chocks on the bottom of the deck high and dry. We were ready for business. We had gone into the dry dock just after dark, and by daybreak, we were moving out. The enemy was still mad, and we were not anxious to be caught in dry dock during a daylight raid.

There was much more work to be done. Our crew was accustomed to chipping paint and working at other jobs. But, the long-handled barnacle scrapers were another type of job altogether. Barnacles hang tough and are difficult to remove. The scrapers make and break blisters even on a sailor's hands.

Laffey's maintenance and repair work was completed about February 8th and we had received a new coat of gray and blue camouflage paint. The ship now resembled a confused zebra, but

she was beautiful to my eyes. This was my home. I really cared for the Lady. Most of us thought it about time for a rest and even some kind of celebration. But it was not so. There was no rest scheduled for Laffey or her crew. Instead, we were scheduled to depart from Ulithi on February 10th, 1945.

Admiral Halsey's fast carrier groups had returned to Ulithi on January 25th, and Halsey had surrendered command to Admiral Raymond A. Spruance. Task Force 38, the Fifth Fleet and Laffey were assigned to it. We were to be a part of Task Group 58.4, one of five such groups under Spruance's command. Laffey's crew was proud of their blisters now. TD 58.4 was fast, and we would all need all the speed we could get to keep up. Barnacles grow on a ship's hull similar to oysters growing on the sea floor. As the barnacles grow, they begin to drag in the water, and the ship loses speed and power. It is very important to keep them scraped off, so our work would prove rewarding in the coming assignment.

Task Group 58.4 was made up of seventeen destroyers, aircraft carriers Yorktown (CV 10) and Randolph (CV 15), light carriers Langley (CVL 27) and Cabot (CVL 28), two modern fast battleships North Carolina and Washington, and the light cruisers San Diego, Biloxi and Santa Fe. Indeed, TG 58.4 alone was more powerful than what was left of the whole Japanese Navy. Japan still had some powerful warships, but Spruance was not interested in them. We were heading for Japan. Our planes would have to knock out as much Japanese air power as possible. Iwo Jima, an island in the Bonin Islands chain, would be our next invasive target.

Iwo Jima lay about halfway between Tokyo and our bomber bases in the Marianas. Le Island was important as a base for fighters escorting our B29 bombers to Japan. It was also important as a base for crippled bombers to land when they could not make it back to Saipan. Iwo Jima was close to the Japanese air bases on Japan itself, and we figured that if those bases were not neutralized, masses of kamikaze would strike our invasion forces at Iwo Jima. The invasion was scheduled for February 19, 1945.

Laffey left Ulithi on February 10 with carriers of Task Force 58 headed for a point sixty miles off the coast of Japan's home island of Honshu. Honshu lay more than one thousand miles to the northwest, but to throw off the Japanese, we headed in a north-easterly direction. We also took this occasion to conduct exercises with the Marines based in the Marianas on February 12th. These same marines would land on Iwo Jima. We hoped that this wide looping right hook would catch the enemy off-guard.

Steaming with Task Force 58 was more than warships. To keep a Task Force like this at sea for weeks on end requires a unique system. In this case, Service Squadron Six, commanded by Rear Admiral D.B. Beary. It consisted of everything from oilers, aviation gas tankers, supply ships, ammunition ships and even escort carriers. These made the long-range strikes against Japan possible. These service ships could replenish our fuel, ammunitions and ship's store while we were underway. The escort carriers could deliver replacement planes and pilots right to the flight decks of our big carriers without even slowing our speed. We refueled twice while underway between Ulithi and Honshu. The second refueling was on February 14th about five hundred miles east of Iwo Jima. From there on, Laffey and the other destroyers would depend on the larger ships for fuel. The service ships must stay to the rear out of range of enemy planes.

As Task Force 58 swept by Iwo Jima, we would give the bombardment group there a little help with shells and bombs. Even as Laffey was entering Lingayen Gulf with the bombard group there, destroyers went to work bombarding Iwo Jima. Those destroyers included Roe, Taylor, Fanning, Dunlap Cummings and Ellet. My brother Carl Cain was a gunners' mate aboard the USS Roe. I knew he was mixed up in the fight out there somewhere, but until now, I had received no word about the Roe. I asked our signalmen to be on the lookout. They finally found him. Destroyer Taylor hit a mine, and Roe, Terry and Porterfield were clawed by enemy gunfire at Iwo Jima. My brother was injured by an exploding shell. Concussion caused bleeding from his nose and ears, and he was sent all the way to the hospital in New Orleans, Louisiana, before the bleeding was stopped. Most of his gun crew was killed. Laffey and Task Force 58 would be back for the invasion.

On February 15th at 7:00pm, Task Force 58 increased speed to twenty knots. This speed would put us at the launch point sixty miles east of Honshu at 7:00am the next morning, February 16th, 1945. The weather worsened, and, by daybreak pm February 16th, it was downright ugly. How could we launch planes in weather like this with a cold, damp, northeast wind? The sea was a dirty, lead-gray color, churning with green rollers topped with white foam. When the rain stopped, here came the snow. Laffey plunged and rolled and actually seemed to enjoy herself. The larger ships were making out much better than the destroyers.

In calm seas, the flight decks of the big carriers are some ninety feet above the water line. The waves were not rolling over these decks, but they were just a little unsteady. We could not see the carriers because of the weather, fog and spray. The visibility was terrible. But, we knew the raid was on and the planes began roaring overhead. The fighters were first, then the heavily loaded bombers. Some of the fighters also carried bombs and rockets. Could they find the targets? We hoped they could. To come this far, and take all this chance, then be unable to do the enemy any damage was unthinkable. It was necessary to stop at least part of these kamikazes, and the best time to stop them was before they left the ground.

The planes began the sweeps over Honshu. By following the conversations between the pilots, the carriers and sometimes Laffey, we in the radio room could get a very good picture of the fight. It definitely captivated my interest. The weather was better over Japan. The pilots could find their targets easily and were keeping the Japanese planes on the ground. The pilots would sometimes get into an argument over whose time it was to attack a Japanese plane either on the ground or rising to make flight. Some of our planes got shot up, and those that were in such bad shape to endanger the safety of the carriers were ordered to ditch, the pilots picked up by a destroyer and returned to the carrier. The weather was cold and the water as well, so nobody wanted to ditch.

One plane came in that was in really bad shape. Only one wheel would lower, a part of one wing dragged and part of his stabilizer was flapping in the wind. The landing officer waved him off and told him to ditch. The pilot made a circle and asked again for permission to land. Again, he was waved off and told to bail out. The pilot made another round and informed the carrier that he was running out of fuel. The carrier radioed back "Don't bring that thing in here! Bail out!"

The pilot acted as if his radio was out. He made another round and radioed the carrier saying, "Clear the deck! I'm coming in!" And he did. I never knew what they did to the pilot for disobeying orders, but they gathered up his plane and pushed it over the side.

After recovering our aircraft, we retired eastward for the night. Our planes had had a good day and hoped that the next day would be better. The Japanese planes had given us very little trouble thus far. Our pilots did a very good job keeping them off us. We steamed eastward for half the night then did an about-face and headed back toward Japan. We had steamed east to confuse the Japanese and kept moving to keep away from the submarines. We would be back in the same launching area by 7:00am on February 17th. We were not finished with the Japanese mainland. Besides the airbases, the kamikaze staging areas, there were manufacturing plants on our target list. We planned to put some of those out of business.

About midnight, the sea really began to show herself. Laffey was plunging and bucking like a wild bronco. We were accustomed to this kind of roller coaster riding. In fact, I really enjoyed it. What bothered me was how we would keep this task force together and apart in a wild sea and in the blackness of the night. Just imagine seventeen destroyers shepherding two large aircraft carriers, two light aircraft carriers, two battleships and three cruisers under those conditions! The large ships were steaming in formation and the destroyers had the formation ringed. As outsiders, we were equally spaced around the large ships. We had made the 180 degree turn and headed back toward Japan as the weather fell apart. We were more worried about a collision of our ship than the enemy. Just when I thought everyone was settled down on stations, our TBS went wild. Two of our destroyers had run together! Ingraham and Barton, both in our Destroyer Squadron 60, were the colliding ships. There was very little damage, but from the noise on the TBS, you would think we had lost a battleship. It took a while to point the blame finger, and in the meantime Laffey was tending three stations in the defense screen.

We arrived on station sixty miles east of Honshu, Japan, at dawn on February 17th. The weather was very little, if any, better than during the night before. Laffey's crew, manning battle stations, watched as the planes took off and roared overhead headed toward Tokyo. At about 10:30am, our first planes began returning. Their reports were not encouraging. Targets were difficult to find and the weather over Japan was becoming worse. By the time we changed course to get into position to launch strikes on the industrial city of Nagoya, it was evident the weather had no intention of cooperating. We were forced to cancel these strikes. Laffey and the rest of the Task Force turned our bows southward. Time had run out. Further attacks on the home islands of Japan would have to wait. Our carriers had launched about eleven-hundred strikes on Japan. We would be needed at Iwo Jima on February 19th, 1945.

The island of Iwo Jima is a pile of volcanic rock and sand about four miles long and two miles wide. There was nothing of

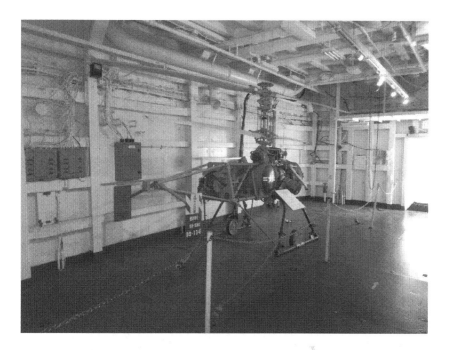

beauty to attract anyone, but Iwo was one of two islands in the Bonin Islands chain that was large enough for an airfield. We must have one of them! Iwo Jima was chosen. The only way to get it was to move in with a force large enough to take it away from the more then twenty-three thousand well-equipped, and well dug-in, Japanese soldiers who didn't want us to have it. The Japanese had the advantage and the high ground. We had a hell of a fight before us!

For ten weeks now, our ships and planes had pulverized those eight square miles of rock and sand. But, as the time for the invasion grew nearer, the bombardment intensified. In addition to the guns, the battleships, cruisers and destroyers, and the bombs form the planes of some twelve escort carriers, Task Force 58 was to roar down with its massive striking power as the Marines started ashore.

Task Force 58 arrived off Iwo Jima on February 18th. Our carriers launched wave after wave of planes against the island. We smothered it with bombs, and we shot at it with every kind of gun we had. The bombardment was so intense that the smoke and dust and flame concealed the island. From a distance, it seemed the whole island was afire down to the water. Even this battering did little good. The natural honeycombed volcanic rock gave perfect protection to the enemy and his guns. Nothing but a direct hit would dislodge most of them, and the Navy with spotter planes ahead took on the job. It would be more than a month before this fight would be over.

After three days of rough seas off Iwo Jima, Laffey steamed north again with Task Force 58. There had been little enemy air activity against our ships at Iwo. During our raids of February 16th through 17th, our planes had shot down or destroyed on the ground an estimated five hundred Japanese aircraft. But, we knew they had several thousand more to use against us. With only about five weeks left before Operation Iceberg, the invasion of Okinawa, we wanted to destroy as many planes as possible. Iwo Jima had not stirred up many kamikazes, but landing on Okinawa would surely bring them out.

Our picket destroyers, well out ahead of the destroyer screen and main formation, were expected to encounter enemy ships and a horde of kamikazes. They found the ships on patrol, but the planes did not attack. This was, and is now, puzzling. There we were, off the Japanese coast for the third day within a week, and they didn't seem to care. Surely they knew we were coming. Maybe that was their way of trying to fool us into believing there would be no resistance at Okinawa.

The weather was bad, about like we had left it on the 17th: cold, rainy, high wind and wild seas. In fact, the sea was so wild, the destroyer Moale, in her plunging and bucking, had her bow to cave in. She was okay, but we were forced to slow our speed.

We reached our launching station sixty miles off Honshu on the morning of February 25th, 1945. Laffey was in the forward screen ahead of the main force. We must have been only about forty-five miles from land. That's really weird. Forty-five miles off Japan's main island Honshu and there was no interference. At 7:00am, our carriers launched their first group of planes. The weather just was not for flying, and by the time these planes returned, the operation was cancelled. Although Japan had suffered terrible damage, they could count themselves lucky. The damage could have been much, much worse had the weather been better. The weather did not get any better, so the strikes scheduled for the 26th were scrubbed. Task Force 58 headed south. There was a job to do at Okinawa.

On February 18th, upon reaching the vicinity of Iwo Jima, Laffey received new orders. We would be detached from Task Force 58, pick some photographs from one of the carriers and deliver them to Guam where they would be passed on to Admiral Nimity's advance headquarters. The materials were needed in a hurry, and to get them, the Navy called on a destroyer, the Laffey, the seagoing version of the Pony Express. As far as I know, no one aboard Laffey uttered a complaint. We were heading away from the kamikazes toward warm waters and sunshine, and the waters were a blue-green instead of an icy gray-green. We were tired of sleet and snow, leaden skies and pounding seas. This cruise would be a pleasure.

The trip to Guan was fast and uneventful. The photographs were delivered and we pressed on to Ulithi, arriving on March 2nd, 1945. We didn't stay long. Within a week, Laffey had her operation orders for Iceberg – the invasion of Okinawa. We would not be running with the big, fast cruisers of Task Force 58 but would be a part of Rear Admiral William H. Blandy's bombardment group to provide gunfire support for the 10th Army ashore. Again, Laffey would be working near a beachhead. The Japanese would have no trouble finding us. That meant kamikazes.

Laffey deported Ulithi on March 21, 1945, as a part of the most powerful naval gunfire unit to back up a troop landing in World War II. Ten battleships, seven heavy cruisers, three light cruisers plus destroyers and destroyer escorts. The firepower of this force was tremendous. Firing broadside, these ships could put more than one-hundred and fifty tons of shells into the air with one salvo. This firepower plus rockets from fifty landing craft plus the bombs dropped by our planes should take care of the Japanese on Okinawa. But, as it turned out, that was not the case.

The trip to Okinawa was uneventful for Laffey. Some of our ships were already in the vicinity of the islands and probably had the attention of the Japanese. On March 23rd, Laffey refueled from the battleship Tennessee while Task Force 58 launched strikes against Okinawa and the Kerama Retto Islands just to the west of Okinawa. Laffey, tied alongside the Tennessee while underway, was a perfect target for the Japanese. Yet, we were not disturbed. We even gathered mail from eleven other ships that same day for transfer toward home. That was a peaceful cruise.

We intended to take the Kerama Retto Islands before the invasion of Okinawa. These islands were too small for airstrips but would furnish very good anchorage for our ships. March 26th was the date set for seizing these islands located about twenty miles west of Naha, the capital of Okinawa. On March 24th, we arrived in the area of Okinawa and began the bombardment of Kerama Retto. We saw no enemy planes on this day. We saw no planes on the 25th although the bombardment continued. Our own places had given the enemy airstrips on Okinawa such a pounding that they were unable to launch enough planes to give us any trouble then or later.

We knew the Japanese still had plenty of planes. Okinawa beaches lie only thirty miles south of the airfields on Kyushu, the southernmost home island of Japan. We were in range of just about every operational airfield the enemy owned, including Formosa (the former name of Taiwan). What were they waiting on? We knew they would be there. While we were enjoying a little respite, Task Force 58 had been busy. We were really in the eye of the storm. The enemy evidently saw Task Force 58 as the core of danger. Even before we sailed from Ulithi, Task Force 58 was again off them coast of Japan pounding airfields. This time they were not so fortunate. Big carriers Franklin, Enterprise and Yorktown had been hit by kamikazes. The Franklin was damaged so badly that she had to be towed out of action. She survived, which was a miracle, but was lost to the remainder of the war. Evidently, Japan had lost more planes than we were aware of. Their attacks on our ships and our attacks on their airfields had cost them dearly. Still, Japan believed they could win. They were counting on their "divine wind," and they thought they could break outback at Okinawa and the war would be over. Even then, the U.S. was planning for the invasion of Japan itself.

The enemy realized by March 26th that we were not going away and began to send their planes against us. At 6:20am, one of our FF54 destroyers, Kimberly, steaming on picket duty north of Kerama Retto, was the first picket ship to feel the cold, furious breath of the Divine Wind. Two kamikazes jumped Kimberly. One plane crashed into a gun mount. Not much damage was done, but we certainly got an awakening hit as to what was to come. Until now, Laffey and bombardment Task Froce 54 had been in the middle as the storm swirled around us. Now, the wind was beginning to shift. No longer would we be ignored. The calm center was shifting. We would be battling the raging force of the Divine Wind. Laffey could maneuver and she could shoot like hell, and it would take all this and more to keep her afloat. Her crew knew this. They were hunched in their battle stations like so many robots, their eyes fastened on the skies and their hands on the ready.

March 27th dawned a beautiful day. But, at 6:55am, this began to change. A kamikaze beat the gunners and crashed on the fantail of light cruiser Biloxi. A few minutes later, a veteran of Pearl Harbor, the battleship Nevada, felt the wrath of the enemy. The enemy was now in our yard. Kaw-lam! High speed minesweeper Dorsey was hit. Dorsey was right over there about a mile away. Ten minutes later, here came another suicider, this one right at Laffey! Those robots, hunkered over those triggers and buttons, became live beings. Wham! Bang! Bam! Rat-a-tat-tat! The fat is in the fire! We have seen this many times, but there's no feeling like that when you see that kamikaze go into a steep bank then come out of it with his nose pointing straight at your ship. The only way to stop him now is to kill him – not the pilot- the plane. There was only a few seconds. Bam! Bam! Ka-bang! Rat-a-tat-tat! Get 'em! You stand with your eyes glued onto him. Exploding shells fill the sky with smoke balls. But, the thing is getting larger as the clock ticks. Tick-tick-tick – wham! Suddenly, our gunners get him. He explodes all over the sky. Laffey is safe for the moment, and we breathe again. The gunners hunched in their positions chew their tobacco and spit their juice. They did their job well. The wreckage of the suicider burns on the water less than a mile away.

For the next few days, we saw a pattern of attacks like this. A few, or even a single plane at a time. Where were the hordes of planes that we were expecting? Judging from what happened later, I believe there was not only confusion in Japan but that they finally decided to wait until we had committed everything to the battle at Okinawa and then send in all they had left. A do-or-die attack. For the next few days, Laffey spend her time screening the larger bombardment ships against air attack and whatever else the enemy had to offer. During the daylight hours, we would come close in to the beaches and shoot-up any enemy targets we could find, then at night we would move out to sea or enter the net-protected anchorage Kerama Retto. We were not too concerned about planes or gunfire from shore. But, the Japanese had lots of suicide boats at Okinawa. Our forces had captured over one hundred of the pesky little rascals at Kerama Retto. These boats were small and fast and very difficult to see close in to shore.

Our forces went ashore on Okinawa as scheduled on Easter Sunday, April 1, 1945. Though there were many beaches suitable for landing, our forces had chosen the Hagushi beaches in the southeastern part of the island. We did not land here, of course, and our only resistance was a few floating mines. We exploded these with gunfire, mostly our 20mm anti-aircraft guns.

Marines of the first and sixth division and soldiers of the Army's seventh and ninety-sixth infantry divisions were landed at Hagushi beaches. Bitter resistance had been expected by the enemy. We thought it would be as bad, or even worse, than Iwo Jima. That's why we brought such a huge bombardment force and had shelled the beaches for a week before the invasion. But, to our surprise, the resistance was very light. Okinawa is sixty miles long and eighteen miles wide at the widest point. There are some forty

beaches we could choose from, and with the bombardment force we had, General Ushijima probably knew he could stop us from landing. He probably decided to take the one hundred thousand troops of his think-second army and try to defend only one heavily fortified part of the island. No doubt General Ushijima knew he could not expect any kind of reinforcements. We had him sealed off from Japan as tight as a drum.

The terrain south of Hagushi is very rough, filled with ridges and high, flat plateaus. Every ridge, hill and mountain is honeycombed with holes and caves in the volcanic rock. Here, Ushijima dug in his army. Here, safe from all but direct hits, his troops waited like spiders to pounce on our troops. Pounce they did. The campaign cost forty thousand casualties on our side. But, we needed Okinawa for a base to support out attacks on Japan's home islands.

Ashore, the Marines turned north and the Army turned south. The Marines met little resistance and within three week had two thirds under control. The Army ran straight into Ushijima's Shuri line and got nowhere in three weeks. This, evidently, was Japan's plan: to tie our landing ships and bombardment ships close to the beach and seas around Okinawa. Here we were targets for the suicide pilots of the Divine Wind. That "wind" was about to blow.

April 6th began like any other around Okinawa. A little hazy with a few clouds overhead. The brisk northeast wind was whipping foam from the tops of waves. This could have been a beautiful picture had it not been for the sights and sounds of war. Laffey was busy about her duty of screening the large ships bombarding the beaches. We kept a distance of seaward watching for planes, submarines and suicide boats. Occasionally, we would find a floating mine. There had been very little activity from the kamikazes, and considering our location, this had been about a routine day.

This condition continues until about mid-afternoon on April 6th, then all hell broke loose. The Japanese had finally decided to do something – they had decided to unleash the full fury of the Divine Wind on our ships around Okinawa. There were ships as far as one could see in most any direction. Buckner Bay, as we had named the area around the landing beaches, was stuffed full of every kind of ship, tankers, transports, LSTs and all other kinds of landing and supply ships. Bombardment Task Force 54 was stretched out for miles – battleships, cruisers and destroyers. The suiciders didn't come singly. They didn't come in pairs. They came in droves. They came like flocks of birds in flight. They pounced on everything they could find.

Our ships fought back. Every gun that could be brought to bear was firing. Smoke from exploding shells soon covered the sky. It was a heavy overcast, but of powder smoke and not clouds. Tracer shells from the anti-aircraft guns looked like sparks going up from a huge bonfire. Yet, the kamikazes came through. The transports, supply ships and LSTs really took a hammering. Also, seven destroyers and one destroyer escort were hit. Our combat air patrols got some of them. Laffey's guns got some of them. But, we could not get all of them. Those planes that did get through our gunfire inflicted more damage than we had suffered since our arrival off Okinawa.

It was estimated that more than three hundred enemy planes of all types attacked our ship at Okinawa on April 6th. More than two-hundred seventy-seven were destroyed either by gunfire or suicide dives. Laffey, from her position on screening station on the southwest perimeter, almost had a ringside seat. Most of the planes came in from the north and northeast and didn't come directly over us. Laffey was not damaged. We had been through this kind of attack many times before, but nothing of such magnitude and intensity. After about two and one half hours, the battle began to die down. But, the smoke didn't clear. It was like we were in a twilight zone. Everywhere you looked, it seemed everything was afire or smoking. Hell had come down to meet hell.

There was no rest or relaxation for Laffey. This was only the first puff of the Divine Wind. The Japanese had more. This raid was supposed to have put most of our ships out of action. Now, the enemy would send what Navy it had left on a suicide mission to wipe us from Okinawa. At 4:00pm on April 6th, 1945, these remaining ships steamed through Bungo Straight between Kyushu and Shikoku and headed straight for the Okinawa beachheads.

The huge and powerful sixty-three thousand ton battleship Yamato, with nine 18.1 inch and twelve 6.1 inch guns, and eight destroyers only had enough fuel for a one way trip. Their mission, called "Ten-Go," was planned that way. The crews of these ships knew they would not be coming back. They were planning to reach our transports and other ships on the beachheads with their destructive power. But, even if they failed here, they hoped to draw our planes away so their kamikazes could be free for another attack.

This effort was tragic, futile and useless. As soon as these warships passed through Bongo Straight, they were spotted by two patrolling American submarines, the Threadfin and the Hackleback. With that discovery, their doom was already sealed. The message from the submarines was received by Admiral Mitscher, and he began immediately to move his task groups into position to intercept them. Admiral Spruance, agreeing with the actions of Mitscher, also directed Rear Admiral Morton Deyo to Okinawa to form a surface attack force and prepare it for battle.

Laffey was a part of Admiral Deyo's force of six battleships, seven cruisers and twenty destroyers. As this huge force was being assembled, Laffey and three other destroyers on the west side of Okinawa were ordered to sail ahead of the main force. They were to catch up to us later. We had the Japanese outnumbered in ships and firepower but it was all behind us. Here our nerves were tested. We plowed north all night planning to attack over the TBS (talk between ships). The Laffey was to make the first torpedo run. I was sweating and I'm pretty sure the whole crew was on edge. The Yamato was out there. We had been close to this monster a couple of times, but now we expected to face her in a few hours. As Laffey raced through the darkness, thoughts were racing through my mind. The once night Japanese Imperial Navy was down this small group about to be challenged by four American destroyers. Could it be possible that Laffey might fire the torpedo that would write finish to the Japanese surface fleet?

The word came down: "Set torpedoes to run at twenty-two feet." This department would place our explosive fish just below the sixteen inch armor plating on the Yamato's hull. But to do that, we would have to get by the destroyer screen, the cruiser and then under the battleship's big guns. I really believe Laffey could do that. The battleship would open fire at twenty-two and a half miles. The cruiser and leading destroyers would be closer to us, but open fire about the same time. Our eyes were for the Yamato. After

evading the destroyers, we would out-maneuver the cruiser then down the starboard side of the battleship. Every gun would be raking the deck of the monster while our torpedo men launched five torpedoes.

Then, over the TBS, "Laffey, if you make it, prepare for a second run."

The tide had turned for the Japanese. They might inflict some damage and casualties on us but they would never make it past us to the beachheads.

At day break on April 7th, Laffey was still plunging north with all that firepower behind us. But unknown to us, far to the south east, three carrier groups were racing for position to intercept the Japanese. At 8:30am, the pilot of a search plane spotted the group, and by mid-morning, two hundred carrier planes were in the air heading toward Admiral Ito's ships. The U.S. planes found Ito's ship about noon. Two and a half hours later, there was no more Imperial Navy.

We were that close! However, at that moment, Laffey witnessed the passing of an era. The sinking of the mighty Yamato by carrier planes meant the battleship would no longer be queen of the seas. The carrier with her planes had emerged as the major ship of our fleet. Laffey never got a shot at Yamato. We may have been able to beat Admiral Ito. At least Laffey would have tried. With a sad note in my mind, we returned to our bombardment station at Okinawa. There was plenty of fighting ahead for Laffey. The war was far from over. We believed the Japanese were whipped, but we knew they were not going to quit. I really thought we would have to invade Japan before it was over.

April 12th, 1945, was not a particularly good day. The view from our side was looking pretty good considering progress that had been made. We had come to Okinawa with the intent of taking this group of islands from Japan and turning them into a fortress against the enemy. We came prepared for whatever we might find to do. Our carrier planes had pounded airfields on the Japanese home islands time after time. We had brought such a huge air force aboard dozens of aircraft carriers that it looked like floating portable airfields. We had enough gun power aboard ships, including floating fun platforms, to level the island. We had seized from the enemy a large protected ship anchorage at Kerama Retto. Our Navy had perfected a radar picket defense around the islands that could give early warning of incoming Japanese kamikaze planes. We had Lt. General Mitsuru Ushijima's troops trapped on the southernmost end of the island. He was surrounded on three sides by waters controlled by our fleet, and in the north by our advancing troops. We thought we had him right where we wanted him.

The case might be, looking from the enemy's side, that General Ushijima had us right where he wanted us. American soldiers daily advancing against Ushijima's Shuri line could be measured in feet. Our warships, transports and supply ships were tied to Okinawa where they were easy targets for the kamikazes. Though our radar picket ships and combat air patrol plane were very effective, and the Marines and Army were bothered little by enemy aircraft, some enemy planes did get through the screen. The kamikazes that did get through directed their attacks on the ships in the water around the island. Evidently, the enemy thought he could knock out our sea power and strand the American troops on Okinawa. Then, the suicidal Japanese could finally win. Had it not been for our picket ships and their covering CAPs, this plan may have come close to success.

As a result, the Japanese began to concentrate many of their kamikaze attacks on the isolated groups of picket ships stationed forty to seventy miles from Okinawa. These massed attacks on the picket ships presented the Navy with a problem. Our destroyers were designed to serve as pickets for just moving naval task forces, or protect bombardment groups. But their high radar masts were needed to spot enemy planes up to sixty-five miles away. There is not much room to maneuver in an assigned station, and when one destroyer is attached by up to fifty planes, all he can do is dodge and shoot. Our losses in ships and men were tremendous.

April 12th was a good day for the Divine Wind. Three destroyers, the Purdy, the Zellars and the Cassin Young, were badly damaged. Also hit were the destroyer mind-layer Lindsey and four destroyer escorts Rall, Riddle, Whitehurst and Walter C. Wann. These ships had been battered. Also, the destroyer minesweeper Jeffers was mauled. Laffey and many other ships around Okinawa had steamed on without a scratch, carrying out our assignments because of the sacrifice of ships on the picket lines.

Laffey would get her jolt at about 8:30pm this same day when we were going about our assignment of screening the battleship New York while she hurled fourteen inch projectiles into General Ushijima's hard-pressed troops on the southern end of Okinawa. Laffey was patrolling around the big battleship on alert for suicide speedboats, aircraft and submarines. The jolt came by way of a radio message. Of course, the message was encoded, and the radioman who copied it had no idea what he had copied. Our communications officer, Lt. Ted Runk, wasted no time in decoding the message. Then, we knew Laffey was ordered to relieve a ship at radar picket station number one. This struck fear in the hearts of every man aboard our ship. We knew what this meant: a confined location, spot the incoming enemy and relay the information to the command ship at Okinawa, then run and fight like hell!

I think that after the initial shock had a little time to wear off, most of the crew began to settle down and think. Thousands of men had heard this same message over the past few days. They took their turn and all had done a fine job. Now, it was our turn. Besides, we had not come to this far away place just to sit and wait for the enemy. We had come to defeat him. Let's go out there and get him!

We were directed to take Laffey into the anchorage at Kerama Retto and pick up a fighter-director team from the destroyer Cassin Young. The Cassin Young had been hammered earlier in the day by kamikazes. A fighter-director team, or FIDO, is a specially trained group, usually five men, who is assigned to a picket ship for the purpose of vectoring our fighter planes in to intercept the attacking planes. This is done with the help of radar and radio.

We steamed into the anchorage soon after daybreak on April 13th. The road stall was crowded with ships, like Ulithi had been when we were through there a month ago. However, there was a great difference here. The ships at Ulithi looked well and happy. But these ships here now were dead and dying, victims of the crazed Japanese effort to win the war with kamikaze attacks. Those attacks were to some degree successful. Hundreds and hundreds of men had been killed, and hundreds of ships destroyed. Still, it would continue.

We moved between the rows of battered, crippled ships as one would move through a hospital ward full of mangled and

crippled casualties. The sight was frightening and depressing. We had been through this before, just not as bad. We had seen mangled ships and dead men at Normandy beaches, three landings in the Philippines, Iwo Jima and here. Okinawa was the worst so far. On every damaged ship, some of our own crew members could see their own battle station charred and splintered where a suicider had hit. This can be very discouraging, demoralizing and depressing. But, Laffey was tough, and her crew was tough. Laffey and her crew would be up to the task. We got lots of advice from some of the sailors on these battered ships. I suppose the best advice was "Shoot hard and run fast."

We picked up the fighter-director team, took on fuel, topped off our ammunition magazines and even picked up our mail from the mail ship. Laffey was as ready as she could be. On April 14th, we steamed out of Kerama Retto under a beautiful clear sky heading north. I was a pleasure cruise, if you could look past the terrible conflict around us. The seas were as beautiful as the skies, and the islands, in their rugged, natural appearance, seemed as jewels in the sparking setting. But for the twenty days we had been in the Okinawa vicinity, very few hours had passed that I was not acutely aware of the sight, sound or feel of the battle around us.

We arrived at the radar picket station shortly. This position was located some thirty miles north of the northern tip of Okinawa. This position, being in direct line between Japan and Okinawa, was the busiest and the hottest of all the picket points. Here, Laffey and her crew would be put to the test. The destroyer minelayer J. William Ditter (DM 31) had been on temporary duty for the past two days awaiting our arrival. No kamikazes had appeared during this period, and we had not had contact on our cruise up here. The crew of the Ditter seemed overly happy to see us. We soon found out why.

The Japanese had certainly not run out of planes, nor pilots, and there was still plenty of those man-guided torpedoes. As the ship we relieved disappeared over the horizon to the south, our captain, Commander Frederick Julian Becton, USN, proceeded to give the crew a pep talk. He began by pointing out that Laffey could not expect to have the same luck as did the ship we relieved. He assured us that we would see plenty of Japanese, that they were men driven by desperation, but men nevertheless. We had seen this kind before. We were going to outmaneuver and outshoot them. He ended by saying that we would be tough, and the Japanese would be sorry they ever heard of the Laffey.

Maybe the pep talk did some good. I think the captain needed to talk and the crew just needed to hear a voice. The hardest part was the waiting for something to begin. Within the hour, it did begin. Our nerves were tested as three bogeys appeared on the radar screen. At the time, we did not have a combat air patrol with us. But, the Bryant, on station there about fifty miles east, did have a CAP. We asked for a loan and they sent them over. The CAPs came charging in and missed the target. Our FIDO team coached them back. By then, the Japanese were in sight. A few seconds later, the word "tallyho" came over the radio as the first Japanese plunged into the sea. Seconds later, one of the American pilots reported that all three planes had been destroyed. That was a good start for our side. When the kamikazes headed for a target, they didn't let anything distract them. They were easy prey for our fighter pilots. When the suiciders came in groups, they most always had fighter cover. This made it more difficult for our pilots. Other bogeys were picked up on our radar that day but did not get close for visual sighting. Our radar operators could watch on their radar screen as our combat air patrols were vectored in for the kill.

Saturday night was calm. No bogeys appeared. On Sunday, April 15th, the sky was blue and the sea very calm. In the afternoon, one of our patrol planes reported a Japanese plane in the water a few miles east of us and requested that we investigate. We steamed to the area and found the plane without difficulty. We put a boat in the water, and they brought back a dead Japanese pilot and some code books and other items that were important to our intelligence men. The dead pilot was brought aboard, and our ship's doctor and pharmacist's mates gave it a good inspection then dumped it over the side. Our gunners sank the plane with gunfire. This incident broke the monotony and routine of an otherwise quiet day. All was quiet on radar picket station number one until about 4:50am on April 16, 1945.

Then, it started. Not with a bang, but with more of a look. At almost 5:00am on April 16th, a bogey flew into our airspace not twenty miles away. We sounded general quarters alarm and went to battle stations. But, the bogey didn't seem to want to tangle with us. He stayed just out of range of our guns, flying around for a while as if he was enjoying himself. Then, he flew away. He must have been a spy giving us a look-over. After all, we were the new guy on the block – or in their fly path. The usual routine was for the ship to go to battle stations one hour before sunrise. Since this bogey got us up a little early, we just kept those positions as the cook prepared breakfast. By the time that first "val" (our name for the the Aichi D3A dive bomber) appeared at 7:44am, everyone had eaten breakfast. That Navy chow does a fellow good. It does a lot to reduce the quiver in the tummy. Laffey's cooks were not likely to be referred to as master chefs, but I never turned down their offerings. Most of the crew complained about the food, but I never heard any of them complaining of being hungry. I didn't notice any lost weight either.

The galley on the Laffey with a mock dinner in preparation.

The "val" came in on our port bow. At six miles, our five inches opened fire. Ka-wham! Ka-wham! Ka-wham! The whole ship quivered and vibrated. We kept firing, and he kept coming.

"Get him, you dumb gunners," came a shout from one of our crew.

Ka-wham! My heart at this point was doing a flip-flop. That Val was doing six miles per minute and we were only shaking him up a little bit.

"Get him," came another shout.

At about three miles and thirty seconds away, he chickened out, dropped his bomb, veered to the right and hightailed it out of there. That bomb threw a geyser of water two hundred feet into the air and was close enough to shake us up. That was too close for me.

At 8:20am, bogeys appeared on the radar screen. It was a large formation of bogeys, and they were coming fast from the north at maximum speed! Laffey maneuvered like we have never maneuvered before. We had to move fast and keep them broad on the beam. We were up against a bunch of fanatics from a fanatic nation that was ruled by fanatic leaders. We must keep them broad on the beam so we could bring the greatest number of Laffey's guns to bear. We contacted delegate base at once. This was the USS El Dorado, Admiral Turner's flagship, back at Okinawa. They would send fighters to help. Fighter planes were needed to intercept this huge oncoming bogey formation. And let me tell you that it was huge! The sky was full of planes, and with our fighters flying to intercept, the dots on the radar screen looked much like a freckle-faced boy with a good case of measles. Unbelievable! The news petrified this veteran crew.

"Look at that," one of the crew pointed. The dots were growing larger in the blue skies as visual contact was made. "Here they come!" They were coming all right, and with a vengeance.

A few seconds later, the kamikazes were close enough for identification. The time was 8:30am on April 16th, 1945. The first four suiciders in the lead were four vals. They were rather easy to identify because of their fixed landing gear. Those four split into two pairs with on pair heading toward Laffey's starboard bow.

"Left twenty-five degrees rudder," yelled the captain. Then when the nearest pair of Vals swung to the right, he yelled, "Hard left rudder." The helm was left thirty degrees, the maximum. This maneuver would keep Laffey broadside to the Japanese planes.

Now, the vals were within range, and with two quick pushes on the warning buzzer, all of our five-inches opened fire. Wham! Ka-bam! Bam! Laffey shuddered. The noise was ear-splitting. Bam, wham-wham, whoom-whoom! Deadly black puffballs appeared near the planes. Our four forward five-inch guns began to sound like huge machine guns. One val began to come apart. That's good, I thought, give him another one! He disintegrated in a splash in the sea. The second val, hanging tough and getting closer, staggered as he was hit. His nose dropped lower and lower, then he hit the water. There was no time to cheer though. Our guns spun as the second pair of vals veered to the rear and came up astern. The after mount 53 took one val under fire with its two five-inchers. The kamikaze got the full treatment. That was too much for the Japanese. He went into the drink astern of the ship. While trying to stay out of the range of Laffey's guns, the fourth val had come in range of the guns of LCS 51 and LCS 116 on station near us. Those two LCSs did a good job. The Japanese was in the sea shortly.

No relaxing here, however, for there was a "judy" (the code name we had given to the Yokosuka D4Y dive bomber) on the starboard side! I was standing on the torpedo deck just outside the radio room. This judy was low and close and coming fast. The 20 mm's and 40 mm's were getting a workout as they covered this guy with tracers and then smoke puffs as the 40 mm's made hits. Straight for our soft spot it came, amidships and low, right into the Laffey's vital innards. I believe I could see that pilot's goggles, he was so close to me. My next move would be to rush into the passageway when suddenly the judy exploded in a huge cloud of smoke and flame, showering our ship with debris. This would not be the last suicider to point his nose in my direction. It appeared to me that they were aiming straight at me.

Power to the radio room had been interrupted which gave me the opportunity to help instead with shifting 40mm ammunition between the guns on the after part of the bridge. They were really using the ammunition, but the judys weren't finished. There was one dead ahead, very low on the water, hooking around to the port side. The forward five inchers had him under fire, but he kept coming through all that shrapnel. I was on the main deck just aft of five inch mount 52. The noise was ear-splitting. I turned and looked at the plane as he was completing his turn and heading for the ship – the same part of the ship I was occupying! At that moment, the pilot opened up with his machine guns. I counted them – two on each wing. This was no place for me! I plunged aft through the splash guard hatch just as the judy exploded. Not only were the machine gun bullets raking the deck, but a small motor, generator or starter, from the plan slammed into the bulkhead right where I had been standing only seconds before. Some men were wounded by the shrapnel from the exploding bomb and our surface search radar was knocked out. This radar was used to track low-flying aircraft as well as surface vessels. This was a serious loss. Because of the powder smoke in the skies, visual tracking became difficult. The seventh attacker was a val coming in on the port beam. All the guns on the port side that could be brought to bear were firing at it. The val seemed to be aiming at Laffey's five inch mount 53. The gunfire deflected the pilot's aim, and he skidded off the top of mount 53 and crashed into the sea on our starboard side.

Our situation had become serious. Those kamikazes were mean; they were determined to do us in. A judy zoomed in on the starboard beam. This was attacker number eight, and this pilot was determined. He would kick his rudder first one way and then the other. This gave the notion that he was skipping from side to side. But, that didn't fool our veteran gunners. The tracers from he 20mm guns were meeting him head-on, and the black puff balls from the 40mm exploding shells were right where they were supposed to be. The Japanese plane disintegrated and dropped into the sea, carrying the kamikaze pest with it.

Eight down, but upon looking up at the sky, we saw it was full of planes and not all of them were ours. By 8:42am, it already felt like we must have been at this for hours. But, no, it had only been twelve minutes since the attack began. Unbelievable! Our gunners were really putting on a show, and the combat air patrol was doing their part keeping some of the planes off of us. Then, here came another one, a val this time, baring in from the port bow at about five miles per minute. He was not at all bashful but seemed to know what he was doing as he flew down low to the water. Number nine attacker was on the way. Our antiaircraft guns were reaching out for him with tongues of fire. The val wiggled then seemed to shudder as the fire was getting to him. But, he was getting to us. At the last moment, he banked ever so slightly to the right, zoomed over the port side 40mm mount, cleared the stacks and wiped two 20mm mounts off the after torpedo deck. Most of the plane went into the sea on the starboard side. But, it left a trail of destruction. Two 20mm guns were destroyed and two gunners were dead. We were hit! Fire amidships! Fire amidships! Burning gasoline flooded across the superstructure deck. A crew member jumped over the side to escape the flames. He was later picked up.

The firefighters got their first real workout. This was no drill. This was the real thing. The whole area was a mass of flames and wreckage. Laffey was racing through the water. The billowing smoke was being wafted aft. This helped to clear the air, but the heat was becoming intense. The burning gasoline was creeping toward a 40mm mount. Ammunition was stored at ready around the inside of the gun tub. When the fire reached the shells, they began to explode, knocking holes in the deck. This caused a fire problem in the compartment below as the burning gasoline poured through. The flames and damage were serious. We were crippled just a little bit, and the black smoke billowing from Laffey would tell the new to every kamikaze in the vicinity. That didn't take long.

Here came kamikaze number ten. Another val traveling low and straight from the rear. So low and fast it seemed the wash from his propeller was kicking up spray from the sea. He probably took advantage of the trailing smoke from Laffey's fires and was not spotted in time for an evasive maneuver. The responsibility for stopping him fell to the three 20mm guns grouped on the fantail. Those guns opened up with a barrage of slugs that tore chunks of metal from the val. But, it was too late to stop him. He was too close. With a terrible grinding, wrenching crash, the plane plowed through the group of guns, sending men and steel flying, and continued on to impact the starboard corner of five-inch mount number 53 with a bone-jarring, shattering, ear-splitting explosion as the bomb detonated. The 20mm group was wiped out with the loss of six men. One man was killed in mount fifty-three. Fires were raging on the fan tail.

At about 8:47am, kamikaze number eleven bore in from the starboard side, aiming directly at what was left of mount number 53. The starboard five-inch gun was canted skyward. More holes were punched in the main deck. Six more men died. Roaring fire and smoke covered the fantail. At 8:50am, another val, taking advantage of the lack of guns aft, bore in from astern. This was attacker number twelve, but not a kamikaze. Rather than crashing his plane into the ship, the pilot released his bomb, hitting the deck over the ship's rudder. The explosion cut electrical cables and split hydraulic lines controlling the rudder mechanism. The rudder was jammed. The plane flew away untouched.

Two more Japanese planes were sighted approaching our port side. We needed speed, but speed would only fan the fires. The captain made the choice, "Flank speed! Give us everything you have!" Laffey responded. She shuddered and dug in with her screws. With the rudder jammed at twenty-six degrees left, Laffey sped in a long arc trying to shake the suiciders. Every gun that would fire was pouring out a hail of steel, but the kamikazes kept coming, headed for our port quarter. Laffey lunged through the sea, trailing ugly black smoke from her wounds. The sky was filled with exploding shells and laced with tracers, but the planes kept coming as if they were walking in the black puffs of smoke from exploding shells. It seemed an impossibility, but those planes came through that wall of fire and steel put up by Laffey's gunners. The lead plane, kamikaze number thirteen, crashed into the after deckhouse in a huge ball of fire. A few seconds later, the second plane, number fourteen, hit the ship in almost the same spot. Flaming gasoline turned what was left of the after deckhouse into a flaming inferno.

Our Laffey was in bad trouble – really bad trouble. Her rudder was jammed. There were wounds and fires in most of her after spaces. An engine from a kamikaze was lodged in the back of the after five-inch mount and another in the after deckhouse washroom, both red-hot metal. One five-inch mount, six 20mms and two 40mms were out. An incendiary bomb layed exposed in the waste disposal trough in the after deckhouse head. There was wreckage everywhere. Parts of a plane were lodged in the K-gun depth charges. After-berthing compartments were afire. Laffey was like a torch leaving her mark in the sea.

I was in the quarter deck passageway when the loudspeaker informed damage control amidships that two men were trapped in the emergency diesel room. This location was in the after-part of the ship, the last space under the fantail. They had retreated to this space from fire in a berthing compartment. Lucky for them, the telephone was working and they were able to call for help. The only way to rescue these men was to cut a hole in the main deck and pull them out. This required a cutting torch. A tank of acetylene gas was lashed to the bulkhead in the passageway. I grabbed the tank and headed aft on the starboard side main deck. The port side was pretty well-blocked by attackers thirteen and fourteen. I just wasn't quite prepared for what I found as I rounded the starboard deck-housing and came upon the carnage at five-inch gun mount 53 and the wreckage beyond. The fire had been partly contained around mount 53, but the deck was so pitted by shrapnel and bomb explosions that it was necessary to pick my footing

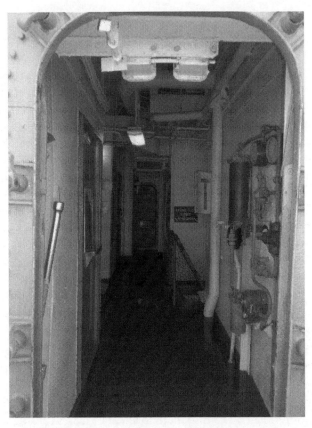

carefully. The five-incher was a wreck, the group of 20mm were gone from the fantail and the roller depth charge rack was a mangled mess. But, worse of all, the twisted bodies of my shipmates were all around me. I really got a shock when I looked up at the gun mount. The sides and back enclosures had literally burst apart. A vertical ladder was used to gain access to the hatch on top of the mount. Normally, the spotter climbed the ladder and stuck his head out of the hatch for visual sighting. However, at this time, the spotter, who was in his usual position, was burned to a crisp! This was the type of picture you never forget.

After delivering the gas tank, there was nothing more I could do here. So, I returned to the radio room to check on things there. We could steam in a circle and shoot, and we were scared and mad. We had no intention of permitting those kamikaze idiots to get Laffey! I was second-class petty officer, and my battle station was the radio room, but since the radio was out, my duty was whatever I could find to do – and that was plenty. I returned to the torpedo deck in time to hear the warning that another kamikaze was approaching. This one was an "oscar", code name for the Nakajima K1-43 fighter which could carry bombs. He came in from the port bow with a different roar, like he was whining just a little bit. Or, some of that noise could have been coming from the American F4U Corsair that was riding his tail. The corsair was flying at a slightly higher altitude than the kamikaze. This gave our 20mm and 40mm a little space to fire at the Japanese. Both planes were moving like bats out of torment. The American corsair was laying the machine-gun slugs into the oscar. This probably spoiled the kamikaze's aim. The kamikaze skimmed over the port side of the bridge and hooked his wing on the yardarm on the port side of Laffey's mast. The oscar went spinning, missing the after-part of the ship and crashed into the sea. The corsair, hot on the Japanese's tail, was unable to pull up in time and clipped the huge "bedspring" air search radar antenna atop our mast. Despite the encounter with the antenna, the corsair pilot fought for control, and as I watched in amazement, he gained enough control to right the plane, shoot skyward and bail out. When I saw the parachute open, I cheered just a little. I am sure that this pilot saved our ship from a horrible crash. The corsair was a part of out combat air patrol arriving to aid us in the fight. My spirits soared, and in my mind, so did the corsair pilot stock.

Though our combat air patrol was in place and really doing a good job, Laffey was far from out of trouble. The CAP was knocking Japanese right and left, but they could not get them all. Rather than fight back, the kamikazes would do their best to maneuver around the American planes and aim for Laffey. To demonstrate the point, kamikaze number sixteen was on his way coming in from the port beam. Our 20mm and 40mm opened fire on the judy. I was on the main deck port side just aft of the five inch mount 52. When the twin 40mm gun on the deck above me opened up, I whirled to look at the plane. Just then, the Japanese opened fire with all four of his machine guns, two on each wing. Those gun flashes were as bright as stars, and I was definitely in the wrong place. I headed aft as the slugs began to impact against the superstructure and the bulkhead right behind me. I dived through the hatch in the splash guard under the port 20mm. The judy was already in trouble as a corsair was really filling him full of holes, and the 20mm and 40mm added to his problems. Just as I went through the spray shield, the judy hit the water with a tremendous explosion, showering Laffey with shrapnel. The explosion was only about fifty yards away, a real close near miss. Shrapnel tore through the thin steel door of mount 52, injuring several men inside. A few minutes later, I was back up the deck by mount 52, and laying there on the deck was an electric motor or probably a generator from that Japanese plane. It had hit the bulkhead under mount 52 about four feet above the deck, just about where I had been standing when I saw the gun flashes from the kamikaze a short few minutes before. The American corsair had banked left and crossed our bow at high speed.

The seventeenth attacker was approaching from the starboard side. He was hugging the water and aiming at the superstructure. The 20mm and 40mm on the starboard side went into action, and the plane was splashed some distance from the ship. This distraction opened the way for attacker eighteen who was lying back off the starboard beam. The spotters in mount 52 spotted him first. He was a long way out, but we knew that would change fast. Mount 52 trained their guns to starboard as fast as they would spin. As soon as the kamikaze came into range of the five-inchers, mount 52 opened fire. The plane was so low on the water that he looked almost like a motorboat. The first salvo from mount 52 fell short. The suicider seemed to come right through the wall of water hurled skyward by the shells. Mount 52's gunners adjusted the range and fired again. This correction was just right. The five-inch shell hit the Japanese plane straight-on in the propeller. The shell, plane and bomb exploded in a high fireball. That was all for attacker number eighteen.

While mount 52 was eliminating attacker eighteen, mount 51 was training to starboard to assist when the trainer sighted another enemy plane at about three thousand yards. Mount 51 commenced firing on the second plane, and with little fanfare, splashed the Japanese val more than a mile from the ship. Following this demonstration in shooting, we enjoyed a short lull. Our CAP were still active and I guess they were slowing the flood of the kamikazes. The lull was short-lived as another val approached from dead astern aiming for the already demolished fantail. This was attacker number twenty. The pilot had used the sun and the thick cloud of smoke trailed by Laffey to hide his dive bomber until the last minute. He did not crash his plane into the ship but dropped a bomb that further ripped the already-battered fantail. The val continued low over the length of the ship and appeared to be headed home, but about five hundred yards off our bow, he was bounced by an American corsair and went into the sea. He hit us but he paid for it.

I was forward and one deck below the mess hall in my berthing area when kamikaze twenty-one was spotted. Forward five-inch mounts 51 and 52 commenced firing. But, the Japanese kept coming. The pilots had no intention of bailing out, so, the only way to stop or turn the plane was to splatter it, make it explode or shoot off a wing. Seems like the five-inchers could get them, but kind of like quail shooting, a near miss didn't bother him. When I heard the guns open fire, I immediately headed topside. I had to run forward through the crowded berthing area, up a ladder to the mess hall then aft through the mess hall to the port ladder that would take me t the main deck. By the time I reached the mess hall, the starboard 20mm and 40 mm had opened fire. I know the plane was on the starboard bow. I think the Japanese had

a personal grudge against me, but I can't figure how they seemed to know my location.

I increased me speed as I passed through the mess hall, and just as I reached the ladder…Kaw-Bam! The mess hall was filled with shrapnel, chunks of metal, some and just about anything else that would move. I'm sure that what saved me from injury or worse was that half of the huge, round steel mast pole that protruded into the mess hall in the center of the ship. The explosion was in the starboard corner, and I was at the ladder in the port corner and shielded by half of that eight-foot diameter pole. The attacker had come in on a long glide from the starboard bow, strafing as he came. The 20mm and 40mm were eating him alive, but he managed to pull up enough to go over the bridge, and as soon as he pulled up, he released his bomb. The bomb exploded in the 20mm gun nest below the starboard wing of the bridge. Two guns and two crews were on this platform. The guns were destroyed and the men were all killed or wounded.

This is the same bomb that blew through into the mess hall. Also, it blew a huge hole in the wardroom which was being used as a hospital by Dr. Matthew Darnell. One pharmacist's mate was killed and several men wounded, including the doctor. Several of these wounded were in the wardroom for treatment of wounds received early in other parts of the ship. The pilot that had dropped the bomb tried to pull up after he cleared the ship, but he never had a change. An American corsair pounced on him like a hawk on a chicken and shredded the val like he was paper.

While we were trying to deal with the damage caused by the bomb, kamikaze number twenty-two was awaiting the opportunity to dive on the wounded Laffey. We were in trouble, even to the point of sinking. But, we still had a few guns and a little maneuverability. Laffey looked like a torch, trying to defend herself, trailing smoke and flame as she sped in a huge circle of twenty-seven degrees to the left. She was hurt and appeared to be dying. The suicider off the port bow had made up his mind to deal the death blow and began getting closer with each second. The pilit picked his spot – the port side of our bridge. He seemed to be aiming at the pilot house. I think he was looking for unmanageable territory to strike at. There was not much choice left. I just could not believe this thing that was happening to our ship. Laffey was supposed to fling torpedoes and shells and depth charges and run like hell. She was never designed to take punishment like this.

The port 40's and 20's took on the judy with a hail of metal, and the judy took on our gunners. The Japanese slugs were splattering against the gun shield of 40mm mount 42 as the gun's 40mm shells began bursting against the plane. Suddenly, the strafing stopped. The Japanese pilot probably never saw the corsair boring in on his port side. Again, our CAP had prevented the kamikaze, the Divine Wind, from crashing Laffey. The plane and bomb hit the water a short distance from the ship with a mighty explosion, sending up a mountain of water, showering Laffey with shrapnel and debirs. My good friend and key radioman on my watch, Donald Carter, RM3/C, had just stepped out to the deck from the wardroom, where he had been treated for wounds and had aided the doctor with treatment of other wounded, when the shrapnel hit the ship. Jagged metal whizzed around Carter clanging against the bulkhead. Thinking he had escaped injury, Carter took a few steps on the deck but then collapsed. Carter had not felt a thing, but they picked thirty-seven pieces of shrapnel out of his body. He recovered and went home in ok condition.

Now, our situation had reached the critical stage. Laffey was well down by the stern with her after-spaces flooded. Fires were still burning, the jammed rudder kept us on a circular course and many of our guns were smashed. We were far from ready for the next attacker. Fortunately, there were no attackers in sight. There were planes in the area, but they were ours. Back at Okinawa, the command ship was aware of our plight and had sent us a double portion of protection. The Japanese kamikazes had fled for the time being. Maybe we would have a little breathing room and time to prepare for the next attack. The Japanese were very close to victory over the Laffey. Would they quit now?

Our damage control parties were working very hard to bring the fires under control and they were slowly winning. But, the hull was holed below the waterline, and our pumps were unable to keep up with the flooding. We needed help in a hurry. Our command ship had already dispatched two seagoing tugs to help, but they were a long way off. Our radar was out as well as most of our radio equipment. We would be of no value on the picket station, so we would be withdrawn. In the meantime, we must keep Laffey afloat.

Our casualties were being processed in the areas from the wrecked wardroom all the way to the quarter deck. Thirty-two of my shipmates were dead and seventy were wounded – many with critical and very serious injuries. Some few crew members had jumped overboard to avoid fire or were blown over the side by explosions. All were rescued and accounted for. The clean-up continued with one eye to the sky. The lull in attacking kamikazes was welcome but not expected to last long. The Japanese had not given up. While we were enjoying a lull, other ships on other picket stations were under attack by different groups of the Divine Wind. We were very much at war.

I joined a group of men on the quarter deck and we began moving aft on the port main deck clearing out wreckage. Most of the fires were out by now, but the steel was still hot. Parts of Japanese planes and wreckage they had inflicted were everywhere. We cleared the decks and passageways by pushing the debris over the side. The further aft we moved, the worse the destruction. As we reached the after-deckhouse where three planes had crashed in a small area, the boatswain's mate heading our group, in a humorous mood, called out "Ok, all you body-lovers, over here!" Of course, he was referring to the removal of the dead Japanese pilots embedded in the debris. I don't mean this to sound disrespectful. It was gruesome, pitiful work that must be done. The enemy was dying also. We simply must keep up our morale.

This same boatswain's mate brought a few laughs and even some cheer to the crew a few days earlier. We had lowered a boat to pick up four or five dead Japanese airmen to search them for information. The crew had brought the boat alongside Laffey while the search was conducted. The bodies were a little stiff and our crewmen had sat them on the boat seats. The boatswain's mate was in a squatting position in front of one body in the act of cutting the flying suit when a wave caught the boat, giving it a good pitch. The motion caused the dead Japanese to fall upon the boatswain's mate as if he was giving him a big hug. The started sailor frantically fought his way clear of the body. This was a grim but comical situation. I think the crew was actually cheering for the dead Japanese in that little tangle.

Anyway, our gruesome job continued. There were bodies to be removed. Some were identifiable and some were not. One plane had crashed into the after-head, or wash room, and the dead pilot was sprawled across the waste-water trough in the head. The LCS51, on station with us, had come alongside Laffey to help fight

News photo of Laffey's damage. This photo is on display inside the ship at Patriot's Point.

News photo of Laffey's damage. This photo is on display inside the ship at Patriot's Point.

our fires. She also aided in some of our litter removal even though she herself had been hit and damaged as well.

By now, our stern was so near underwater that, had the sea not been calm, we would have been swamped. The sea was the only thing that had been good to us. She had remained calm since we reached station one. Now, any rough seas would most likely sink Laffey. About the most noise that could be heard now was our combat air patrol planes overhead and the constant churning of the water pumps, and the pumps were losing. I left the clean-up crew and joined the pump crew. The suction pipes were equipped with strainers on the ends to prevent debris from entering the pumps. The strainers were clogging with the fiber glass insulation blown out by the explosions and by other debris. I took my turn in the waist-deep water in the lower compartments pulling the debris out of and away from the strainers. Our only option was to pump or sink.

At about 2:30 in the afternoon of April 16, 1945, the two seagoing tugs reached our location and began placing larger pumps aboard and preparing to take us in tow. The sky remained free of enemy planes, but we were some sixty miles from Kerama Retto anchorage. We could make only about four miles per hour under tow, so, we were a long way from any sense of safety. At 3:30pm, the rescue ship PCER 851 hove into sight. This was like a small hospital ship. They came alongside Laffey and took off the wounded, then sped away to transfer them to a regular hospital ship. Soon, it became apparent that the flood waters were beginning to gain on our pumps. We requested more pumps from the tugs. The tugboat USS Tawakoni dropped back and secured our port side near the stern and, instead of giving us more pumps, the tug passed her suction hoses over into our flooded compartments and used her powerful pumps to suck the water out. Little by little, we began to gain on the flooding. Laffey's stern slowly, very slowly, began to rise up in the water.

Our jammed rudder was causing towing problems. Finally, to keep the ship headed in a straight line, Laffey backed her starboard engine and went ahead one-third standard on her port engine. With one engine forward and the other backed, we equalized the jammed rudder problem and we could make about four knots per hour. The seas remained calm and the weather stayed clear all the afternoon and night. Our condition had improved ever so slightly, but a rough sea would surely send us to the bottom. Nobody thought about relaxing. You can't do that on a tin can that is barely afloat in enemy waters.

We did have a little time to think. I suppose I stored a thousand memories of that troubled day on radar picket station number one. For instance, I kept hearing in my mind the whine of the Japanese aircraft engine which sounded like automobile racers. The general quarters alarm sounding "twang-twang-twang," a very mournful warning of possible impending doom. That sound still runs a chill down the spine. The sight of the kamikaze coming almost straight at me, so close I could see the canopy over the cockpit, the engine cowling and the whizzing propeller, exploding at the last second. The plane that banked in on the port bow strafing the deck as I ran for cover. The roar of the five-inch guns, mixed with the chatter of the 20 mm and the stuttering of the 40mm. The vibration of the whole ship from the firing of the five inchers. The acrid smell of powder smoke. The dead and wounded laying about the quarter deck. These are a few of the many memories written in my mind of that fateful day, April 16, 1945. Fifty enemy planes were in the area of Radar Picket Station Number One on April 16th. At least thirty-nine of those planes were involved in the attacks on the Laffey. Twenty-two planes made suicide attacks on the ship – all were destroyed. All were carrying bombs. Nine planes hit the ship. Six planes crashed aboard with their bombs. Three planes hit glancing blows and crash into the sea nearby where their bombs exploded. Some damage was caused by these near misses. At least two bombs were dropped by other planes that scored direct hits aboard.

Early morning on April 17th, Laffey eased into Hagushi Harbor, Kerama Retto, at the end of a twin tow. Even here, in the harbor of the dead, Laffey presented a hideous sight. Survivors of earlier "Kikusui" attacks gazed in amazement at the tortured newcomer. In many cases one kamikaze, hitting in the right place, would sink a ship. Yet, here was Laffey, battered and mangled, making her way to anchorage, having absorbed all the punishment that the Japanese were able to deliver on Radar Picket Station One, April 16th, 1945.

It seemed impossible, but we were in this same anchorage only three days earlier. The scene had changed but little. There were now more ships – more battered ships. On April 14th, we were gawking at the battered, twisted, burned out hulls of battle-damaged ships as Laffey headed out to Radar Picket Station One. Now, on April 17th, the repair parties and crews of those same ships were standing in awe as they gawked at Laffey returning from picket duty at the end of a tow. Battered, blackened, twisted, badly haled aft of mid-ship, guns upended, parts of Japanese kamikazes imbedded in the wreckage, listing to starboard and down by the stern. The miracle was that Laffey had returned at all. Even in her condition, Laffey was riding proud, the few guns left were manned and ready, her crew was busy about their duties, her power plant still working. Only her rudder was still jammed, or else Laffey could have come in under her own power.

Veterans of a two-ocean war, we were no longer scared by the tales of the horrible weapons the enemy had to offer. We now knew all about kamikazes, and the fact that men from other ships could look at Laffey, here off Okinawa, not only told the horror of what we endured, it told them that Laffey could not and would not die. She was strong, a force to be reckoned with, a great Lady who held her own among all the rest. She made me proud to serve on her..........

So, as I headed to Pearl Harbor on the first leg of my journey home, though I held a guilty feeling knowing that I was headed home alive and well while many of my shipmates were not so fortunate, and though the memories of the carnage I witnessed would stay forever etched in my mind, I also felt a sense of pride for what we accomplished. I felt proud for the men who served with me, the ones who sacrificed themselves for their loved ones back home. Every man on that ship gave all he had for her cause, and every one of them deserved honor for that. But, one such being deserved honor even more so.

I looked to heavenward, and I realized that the very fact I stood here breathing and intact was not because of the Laffey and her strength to survive. It was God himself who saw me through this. It was He who protected me, who kept me safe from the blasts, and because of Him, I was alive to share this story with my family and my grandchildren some day. Through every encounter and with every ounce of fear I experienced during this entire ordeal, I knew in my heart that, come life or death, God would see me through and never leave my side. I never let go of my faith, and to this day I hold fast to it. Even faith the size of a grain of mustard seed can move mountains. I know this to be true as I witnessed it first-hand keep an entire ship from sinking regardless its war-torn damage. I still keep that faith today. For just as Laffey could not die, neither can the love our Father in Heaven.

I can only hope and pray that the strength and patriotism these men showed during this nightmarish battle will live on to teach future generations of officers and soldiers. May the courage of this heroic crew set the example to teach the future officers of our country about sacrifice and true patriotism, and may they also have courage and pride for their country and service. May they also have faith in God, and in the end, may they also keep that faith alive.

ABOUT THE AUTHOR

Kevin Cain has lived in Alabama all his life, growing up on the wonderful Southern storytelling, folklore, and traditions. A lifelong fan of storytelling and folklore, he was inspired at a young age to put his stories on paper. The greatest inspiration was listening to his grandparents spend hours telling stories of growing up in the old South. Kevin now resides in Birmingham and continues to pass on the wonderful stories he grew up listening to. His published books and novels include *Thanksgiving Hen on a Chicken Shed: Stories My Grandmother Told Me*, *The Legends of Indian Narrows: Ghostly Childhood Memoirs*, *Haunts*, *Patty Doll*, *My Haunted Collection*, and *Tammy Baby*

http://www.kevincain.webs.com/

Made in the USA
Columbia, SC
18 May 2017